NIGHTMARES
AND SMILES

NIGHTMARES AND SMILES

The Memoirs of a Child Survivor

Mary Natan

To order additional copies of this book, contact:
Xlibris Corporation
1-888-795-4274
www.Xlibris.com
Orders@Xlibris.com
39181

In memory of the Innocent Souls
Murdered by the Nazis

A Few Words by Way of an Introduction

Mary Natan's memoirs of the Holocaust, aptly entitled Nightmares and Smiles, is a gem of a book, though a heart-wrenching one. It is also a homage, as the author states in her dedication, to those "innocent souls who were murdered by the Nazis."

She tells her story, set in a straightforward and unadorned style, with no exclamations, no expletives, no tirades. She does not explain, she tells what truly happened. Her indictment of the Holocaust is made that much more powerful by the restraint she uses in her narrative. Indeed, it almost sounds as though you were actually hearing it straight from the mouth of a ten-year-old little girl, who witnessed the horrors and felt the pain, her own as well as the pain of her loved ones. She was a girl who, though she might have been sometimes scared to death, was never fainthearted, was never broken; she strove on, determined to survive and help others to survive that man-made hell on earth. And for her survival, she had the models of her mother and father who went down fighting for their lives and for the lives of their fellow Jews and all other inmates in those ghastly concentration camps.

How does the heroine come across from the pages of the book? She is a little imp of a girl, precocious, observant, full of inexhaustible energy and intelligent curiosity, full of resourcefulness, determination, honesty, bravery (of the kind you would expect in a boy); a girl with an agile mind who could immediately perceive what was just, unjust, or outrageous; a girl who, though young, understood the importance of living with dignity and believing in the rights of all human beings to live as equals. Another two characteristics, surprising in one so young, should also be mentioned—the young girl's sense of responsibility in those harsh times and her love for her people, one transcending her love for kith and kin.

This book is a page-turner which you cannot put down as one breathtaking scene almost casually flows into another: from the happy scenes of family life in the city of Lodz and then in a village in western Poland where they spent a happy vacation though the dark clouds presaging war, to the mobilization and the outbreak of World War II in 1939; the rapid collapse of Poland and then the Nazi occupation, which led to the establishment of a Jewish ghetto, fenced off form the rest of the city; the misery of trying to survive without the right to leave the Ghetto, to work, to buy, to sell, to go to school, the difficulties of finding food or water, firewood or coal to keep from freezing in sub-zero temperatures; and then there are the occasional sparkles of humanity from Germans and Poles, who themselves were not yet suffering deprivation, and the most striking of all: the good humor and the jokes that went round despite the appalling hardships. Scenes such as these keep the story rolling and hold the reader in suspense. The story moves from camps in Poland to Bergen-Belsen and then to a factory in Eastern Germany. We witness the inhuman cruelty and sadism of the guards (both male and female), the trials of starvation and exposure, and at last the joy of seeing the factory and the railroad tracks bombed by the American planes; and finally the liberation of the survivors by the American troops. Then comes the tragic-comical life of the young Jews moving from town to town in Germany in the hope of finding their relatives alive; many scenes are told with a good deal of humor as there are many escapades and pranks that the author was involved in.

It might be interesting to note that Mary Natan's Nightmares and Smiles has something that comes across from beginning to end—it is the sense of truthfulness, the sense of disbelief that events should have taken such an unspeakably horrible turn, disbelief that ostensibly civilized people could have acted like savages, that so many succumbed to an ideology inciting hate, torture and murder. On the other hand there are the reassuring acts of Jewish people who, after their liberation, refused to exact revenge on their torturers.

Historic periods are characterized by certain ideas of order and of conduct, some seen as right others as wrong and according to those ideas societies mould their behavior. What would be wholesome for the reader to take away from this account of a repugnant political system at its nadir is that the hearts of children should be the pointers of our social and political future because their minds are free of unjust and noxious political ideas and that the indiscriminate tyranny of war must be resisted by the older generation so that inhuman ideas may not take root in the soil of a country which may then lead to the annihilation of millions of innocent people and the wastage of enormous resources. Such totalitarian regimes have achieved nothing but the shackling of freedom and goodness over protracted periods of darkness.

Such inhumanity must never be allowed to come to power in the world—that seems to be the message of this magnificent and inspiring book.

This is, really, a book to be read mostly by the young, for it is the voice of a young girl addressing the present and future generations throughout the world with words of warning.

Educators should make this book recommended reading in schools and colleges throughout the country and it would be wonderful to see it translated into many languages. I believe it will have a humbling and civilizing effect on those who read it, both young and old.

I write as one who comes from Bulgaria, a nation that saved its 48,000 Jews during WWII, because not all stood back in fear of the government that was allied to Germany. In 1943, many groups protested publicly against the planned deportations of the Jews to the death camps and Poland: the head of the Bulgarian Orthodox Church and all the bishops, the professional classes, the writers' union, the trade unions, the clandestine parties, some members of parliament, and finally King Boris III, who in the end did not sign the deportation order. There was another instance, when in 1940 a junior Bulgarian diplomat in Paris saved Jewish Bulgarian lives by arranging, against all odds, a train convoy to transport them to their homeland and survival. That diplomat was my father.

Standing up for one's belief in common humanity can change the world for the better.

Professor Bogdan Atanasov
Los Angeles, March 17, 2007

Who's To Blame?

My Lord, my God thou witnessed the fires raging.
The smoke that billowed, the ash that blew
and sparks that flew straight up to you.

The earth was soaked with blood of victims,
young and old so innocent.
Was all this done with your consent?

Yet from all the nations you choose us with this proclamation,
that as your children did us select
thou in our dire need you did deflect.

Did you not hear those people cry?
Beseech for mercy, pray, say the SHMA.
Our Lord our Saviour we did implore, no more!

My hair grew white, my tears were decimated.
From this lament my hands, they shake
and chains that bind me to the past I cannot break.

My soul's in torment, I dare to ask,
ere when I sleep or lay awake,
"Why did you, all my loved ones take?"
And so I question, I contend, who is to blame?
 Who bears the shame? The sightless weapon or the arm,
that inflicted the pain, and all that harm.

—Mary Natan

1

My name is Maniusia Rybowski. It was 1939, the year of my tenth birthday. That's when I began to be cognizant of myself, my family, and the world around me.

I was the youngest of five children, three brothers and one sister. Steve, the oldest, was fourteen years my senior. Next was Irene, eight years older. David was six years older, and Zenek was four years older than I. We were a close and happy brood. Our home was the one where all the cousins loved to spend their free time. Consequently, the house was always full of young people. As the baby of the family, I was spoiled and pampered, especially by Irene, who acted as a substitute mother.

Our mama kept busy caring for the family and entertaining friends. Dad was a dancing teacher who owned a school and a nightclub. His profession demanded that he be a social butterfly. His life was filled with parties, which he loved to give and attend. He had many friends, and all of them were Poles of German descent—the crème de la crème of Polish society.

That April, my parents gave me a lavish birthday party. All my friends and schoolmates were invited: my best pal Halinka Olsaniecka, whose mom was a doctor, at that time a huge accomplishment for a female; Sarenka Gerson, a real beauty whose dad owned a textile mill; and Ada Hamburska, whose parents were divorced. Her dad resided in Paris, France. He owned a limousine and had a chauffeur who used to pick up Ada for her visits with him. Then there was Maniusia Friedman, whose parents owned the best bakery in Lodz. Often, after class, we would go there for the delicious pastries.

My party was a great success. I received lots of presents, mostly books, for everyone knew that I was an avid reader. Beside the gifts from friends, I got lots of clothes from my parents' friends and my relatives. But the apex of the party was the gift Irene had given me. It was a most beautiful sheepskin coat, with fur on the inside and outside. The outside was embroidered with colorful silk threads, and it came with a little hat, which was the height of fashion. It was every little girl's dream. All in all, it was the best party I ever had.

Besides my party, I loved Christmas. Each year, we were invited to my dad's best friend Erwin's parents. Erwin gave us our beloved dog Lalka (doll in Polish). We all called him Uncle, and we loved him dearly. His mom and dad were very gracious to us and always had gifts for everyone under the Christmas tree. We were considered family, even by the rest of his siblings.

Unfortunately, that year Erwin became ill. No one knew what kind of malady befell him. My father took him to a prominent Jewish physician, who diagnosed it as cancer in his stomach. Erwin's older brother and parents refused to accept the doctor's findings, and for the first time, my dad heard them refer to the doctor as "a Jew."

Erwin's family took him to Vienna to an Austrian medic. Hurt by the remark, my father stayed away, and I wondered if we would spend that Christmas with them. When I expressed my fear and disappointment, dad explained that it was not important. What mattered was Erwin's health, and Dad worried about him. But I happened to overhear my parents discuss the remark they made, especially what his brother had said about "the Jew doctor."

One day my dad was summoned to his bedside. Erwin refused to eat or drink. He became emaciated and demanded to have my dad there. Dad prevailed upon him to consume a little broth. The family resented the fact that he ate from his hand. Erwin died in my dad's arms.

I, too, felt the pain my parents felt about Erwin's death; more so when I heard my dad's disappointment with the whole family, who referred to him as the "Jew friend." Yet all this did not awaken my parents to the terrible anti-Semitism brewing in Polish society.

2

For me, the world was still a happy place, especially that summer when we went away to a small village named Hulanki. We always spent the whole season there, year after year. My parents rented a villa whose owners were also of German descent, as was the farmer who moved our family every summer. He was the father of my friend Lucy; her brothers Arnold and Hans were friends of David and Zenek's.

The farmers used to look forward to our arriving, since Mom made sure that every time we came, she brought shoes the boys outgrew, some soap, and lots of sugar, which was too expensive for the farmers. My dad used to refer to it as the three gifts of the Magi.

Hulanki. The memories of that place still bring a smile to my face. The name alone tells all. In my native language it means a good, festive time. The village was small and very rural. There were no indoor bathrooms, only outhouses, no running water, and no electricity. There were wooden floors, which we covered with wood shavings. Evenings, we lit kerosene lamps, but mostly we sat in the garden, where the women would congregate and relate old wives tales, which to us children were fascinating and, at times, scary. We loved to listen to those stories. Then there was the veranda—what a great place! It was the hub of daily activities. It substituted as a living room, a dining room, and when it rained, a playroom.

On Fridays, Mom would bathe us in a big barrel, which collected rainwater, and to it she would add some boiling-hot water. All this was in preparation for the weekend, when our dad would come.

Dad's work kept him in the city all week long, but his weekends were for family. Dad would arrive by train. Besides goodies for us children, he often brought friends. Thus, even in the country, our home was always full of people. On Saturdays, the grownups would socialize at the club, where the men played cards. The ladies joined the children in the forest, where we picked berries and mushrooms. We also had a man-made lake and a man-made island, where we lay in the sun and enjoyed the company of other children. It was great fun to swim and to ride the boats and kayaks.

We looked forward to Father's visits. Since Hulanki had no station, he would get off at a place called Justinof, which was about three kilometers away. Dad would then take a "briczka," a horse and buggy, and we would hike there and wait for the train. It was fun to see the spitting, noisy locomotive, always exciting. I remember the time when Dad refused to hire the buggy. Instead, he told us that we had to walk, for he had an important secret to tell us, which would take a while. Curious, we pestered him the whole way, but he insisted that we wait until we reached the village. Unbeknown to us, Dad was warned by his doctor that he had to lose weight; thus, he wanted to hike, in order to accomplish it. Being with Dad was fun; he always had something up his sleeve and was always able to fool us.

On that particular Friday, after the ritual bath, we hiked happily to the train station to await his arrival. Much to our surprise, it was Irene and Steve that alighted from the car. Dad was nowhere in sight. Irene attended a fashion school in the city, and Steve was in the Polish army. Irene would come sometimes, but never Steve. He seldom got a pass in the summer. Besides being disappointed, we were curious as to why Steve came but not Dad. When we questioned them, they gave us some story about a new student who insisted on dad's personal attention.

Mom was disappointed, but elated to see Steve. She was proud of her son who was dressed in military splendor, including a saber. She insisted on showing him off to her friends. We spent the whole evening doing just that. The next morning, Mom was in tears when Steve told us that he must leave that night. He explained that he had been given only a two-day pass to visit the family. We could not comprehend why, and that night he departed.

Sunday, I tagged along with Irene as she made visits to her friends. They whispered among themselves. I heard a word here and there, something about a military call-up; all the eligible men had to go. I figured that it had something to do with her Polish boyfriend, who worked for dad as a singer and bouncer at the club.

Next, we paid a call on the Auerbachs, where Irene proceeded to inquire about the possibility of Mr. Auerbach moving the family back to the city as soon as possible. I stood with my mouth opened wide, my heart beating fast. I knew that something awful was taking place, especially when Mrs. Auerbach refused to allow her husband to do so. Never before did that family say "no" to anything we asked of them. I was confounded. What was going on? What was happening? I questioned Irene, but she just hushed me without an answer.

By the time we got home, we were surprised to see Irene's boyfriend Zygmunt, who had arrived while we were out. My mom didn't approve of this alliance, because he was a Gentile, and Mom would rather have seen her with a Jewish boy. This too confused me. I liked Zygmunt, especially his beautiful voice that everyone admired. Zygmunt brought a note from dad saying that he was to bring us home to Lodz safe and sound. There was serious talk about an impending war with Germany. Possibly it had started already, while we dallied. It took two days to convince Mrs. Auerbach to relent and let the Mr. take us back. We packed in a hurry.

3

By the time we were ready to leave, the whole village was rampant with news that the armies were already on the move; ergo, there was no way we could get train tickets. The army was being moved to the front, wherever that was. I had no idea. All I knew about war were tales our mom related. She was a youngster when they had one. Mom was born in Riga, Latvia, where the population was extremely anti-Semitic and blamed every bad thing on Jews. They made a pogrom (whatever that was). Her family fled to Russia while shells were exploding around them. To me it sounded exciting; childishly I looked forward to it.

Then Mom told us that we would have to travel on the cart with Mr. Auerbach, and there was no way we could take our beloved Lalka; she would have to stay. Mom assured us that very soon we would come and fetch her. That stupid war would soon be over; the Germans would be unable to fight against such great armies as the Polish, English, and French combined powers. That was the common belief of all.

At first the buggy ride was fun, until we hit the main road. That was horrible. It was crowded with all kinds of wagons, masses of civilians, and soldiers on foot. If this weren't enough, the German planes paid us a surprise visit. They proceeded to shoot on the hordes of people. Mr. Aurebach decided to pull off the main road where we stopped, hoping to avoid the onslaught.

Now I remember the fear that we all felt. I think that I was shaking and crying. Mom tried hard to keep us calm. If this weren't enough to scare us, the Polish army tried to requisition our transportation, such as it was. Thanks to Zygmunt's quick thinking, we were spared this calamity and retained the horse and buggy. He explained that we were a duke's family, and he, as his aide, was following his master's orders. They bought it hook line and sinker.

Miraculously, we arrived home safe and sound. We got home late. Tired, hungry, and very, very thirsty, we did not find any water. Even if we had, we would not have drunk it, afraid that it was poisoned by our home-grown Germans.

Dad was waiting and very much worried about us. After what we went through, once home, I was excited and could not wait to tell him all about our odyssey. Little did I suspect that this was only the beginning of our trials and tribulations. Mom and Dad were worried about Steve; they had not heard from him since he left Hulanki.

Irene was told by friends that Zygmunt joined the army, which left her broken hearted. She kept checking the daily newspaper, where they printed a list of soldiers killed at the front.

It took only a few weeks for the Germans to conquer the "great" Polish army, whose famous cavalry fought with sabers, riding on their magnificent Arab steeds. The Germans, on the other hand, entered Poland fully motorized. They arrived in Lodz and the rest of Poland on motorcycles and huge tanks, of which "the mighty Poland" had only a few. They entered our city with roars mingled with loud and happy greetings by our own Germans.

Soon afterwards, things began to deteriorate rapidly, especially for the Jewish population. Life began to look dismal. Hordes of young hooligans began to break into Jewish-owned establishments and destroy at will all they could. Next, the Germans ordered people to put out written signs stating that this was a Jewish business. We all were ordered to wear a yellow armband on our sleeves. My dad was told by a German acquaintance that they were rounding up rich Jews and inquiring about him. That night under the cover of darkness, we left the only home I ever knew.

4

My childish notion that war was fun evaporated by the fear I now felt. We moved into the club. My dad reasoned that since the club was now closed, he was sure that they would not think of looking for us there. We left with only the clothes on our backs. With no blankets or any place to sleep, we rested on the floor. In the morning, Dad had the super build a couple of improvised beds in the wardrobe. We had no lights or a place to prepare meals. Our neighbor graciously allowed Mom to use their stove. We paid the caretaker to supply food.

Steve returned. Since he didn't find us at home, he deduced that we were at the club. He escaped a prisoner of war camp with the aide of a Polish nurse, who had given him civilian clothes and some money. She didn't know that he was Jewish. Our happiness of having him alive and with us was marred only by the way he looked. He was quiet, emaciated, and suffering from gallstones.

Irene found out that Zygmunt was interned in a hospital not far from Lodz. He was injured but not seriously. Against my parent's advice, she took of the yellow armband; posing as a Christian, she went to see him.

With Steve's arrival, Mom decided to go back to the apartment in order to get some of his suits. She came back crying bitterly. She found the place ransacked, all our belongings gone. It didn't take long for our Polish "friends" to help themselves to the things they wanted. Dad and Mom went there and removed whatever was left. Luckily, Mom found her silver samovar (a gift from her parents), Irene's sewing machine, and a few other things that she was fond of; mostly things she received from her family that lived in Russia. Then she took those things to her best friend, "Ciocia Lola," for safekeeping.

Dad's money was running out, what with the business closed and paying of the super so he would keep quiet about our living there. Father decided to ask his brother for a loan. Uncle Ruven lived on the same street as we, only a couple of blocks away. He was the oldest of three brothers and very successful.

He and his wife were very frugal. Often they would reprimand my dad for being loose with his money, so Dad felt bad about asking him for help.

It made no difference. When Dad got there, he found them getting ready to move. They had been planning to move to Piotrykof, where he and Dad owned an orchard. They were buying Polish papers and decided to hide for the duration of the German occupation. They proposed that we join them, but Dad was ashamed to tell him that he was broke, much less that he needed a handout. On the way home, he formed a plan. He decided to ask the German authorities for dispensation, in order to be allowed to reopen the club.

The next morning, Dad went to see the German governor of Lodz. Dad's German was perfect. He explained that he was the owner of the best club in the city, and that it would be desirable for the soldiers to have a place to relax after fighting at the front. The governor was amicable. He agreed with Dad and handed him a special pass, which gave Dad permission to reopen the business. Dad was elated; he praised the Germans once more. Two days later, after gathering his employees, he opened the club.

My parents were now happy again. I was not allowed to stay there. My mom arranged with our neighbors for me to sleep in their apartment. I didn't mind, for they had a baby and I loved the tot. I made believe that it was my very own doll.

Once again we were doing well. The club was thriving, money was coming in like before, and Dad was full of praise for the great people. We moved back to our own home.

5

Now that we were back at the apartment, Mom cleaned it up and began to entertain again, mostly officers that my parents became acquainted with. The officers liked a homemade meal, especially my mom's cooking. They said that it reminded them of home.

At first, the Germans would come dressed in their uniforms. Then for some reason, they would show up in civilian clothes. Once dad asked them about it. That's when the soldiers confided to us that they were deathly afraid of the SS men. They explained that to be friendly with Jews was strictly forbidden. At first my dad didn't believe it, but after lengthy conversations, the officers convinced him. They proposed that we go into Russia. They even promised to give us transportation to the Russian front. Steve agreed with them; unfortunately my dad did not.

One busy Saturday evening, two SS men marched into the club. They stopped the music. Guns drawn, they ordered the soldiers to leave. Speechless, my parents watched as the young people left without protest. Next, they inquired who the owner was. My dad stepped forward, holding the permit in hand. They laughed, pulled the paper from his hand, tore it into shreds, and proceeded to beat him viciously as mom watched helplessly, breaking his cheekbone in the process. That was the last day my parents owned the club.

My father was ordered to surrender the ownership to a Polish-German woman whom my dad employed as a cleaning maid. They suspected that she was the one who orchestrated the whole incident. I cried when I saw my dad and ached for him. This was the man for whom the people of our city had a lot of respect. I used to be so proud of him, always immaculately dressed, his fingernails manicured; but now he was a broken human being. The next day we had a visitor, a friend of German extraction. He warned my parents that now was the time to get lost somewhere.

Steve convinced Dad that we should now move pronto. He told Dad in no uncertain terms that he better stop being so naïve and realize that the time has come to fear the "wonderful" Germans. Fortunately, we had just the place to hide, where no one knew us. It was my aunt's apartment. She was my dad's stepsister and very close to Dad. When things began to get bad for us Jews, she and her three children decided to flee to Russia. She gave my dad the keys to her place.

The apartment was spacious, well furnished. It only had one shortcoming; it had only two bedrooms, which all seven of us had to share. I liked sleeping with Irene. The three boys were not too happy to share one bed. My parents were much worse off; they had to sleep in the living room on the sofa. As we settled in, we realized that we brought no food with us, and this was the first time we went to bed hungry.

The super of the tenement told us that there was only one Jewish family left, and that he'd be happy to acquaint us with them. We met the next day, and I was thrilled to find a girl my age. She was an only child. Soon we became friends. Our new neighbors shared with us what little food they had. Afraid to go out, we spent the days playing games. Steve taught us chess, and when we tired of it, he made up a game of war by using the chessmen. It helped us to forget about food until the hunger pains would become unbearable. I would lay down with a book and try not to dwell on it. The boys suffered most. It broke my heart to see them quiet and morose.

David could not abide it any longer. He did go out, hoping to find some food to buy, even though it was forbidden for Jews to enter a Polish store. He was promptly arrested. The official excuse was that they needed men for snow shoveling, but in reality, it was a cruel game they played on the young boys. A man, dressed as a butcher, would enter, pick one of the teens, and leave the room. Suddenly, they would hear a blood-curdling scream. The butcher would reenter, his apron soaked in blood, carrying a sharp knife stained in blood. Most of the youngsters fainted, some even had heart attacks. Dave was the next one chosen. He was taken to a back entrance and told to scream. Then he was released. That was the last time David would venture out.

The Levins decided to leave Lodz. They, too, headed for Russia and asked us to join them. Again, Dad would not hear of it. Irene took off her armband, trying to pass as a Christian in order to by some bread. We waited for her return, hoping that nothing bad would befall her. Suddenly the janitor came; he had bad news for us. While standing in line at a store, his wife witnessed as Irene was arrested by two German officers. Mom was crying and dad was pacing the floor. We children were quiet and very, very scared.

A short time later, we heard heavy footsteps and a loud knocking on the door. Steve opened it, and in strolled Irene, flanked by the two Germans. All three were carrying bags full of provisions. It turned out that the men were friends of Steve's two brothers of German extraction. They had eaten my mother's cooking often and spent many a days in our home. They proceeded to tell us how they spotted Irene in line at the grocery store and made believe that they arrested her. While one stood watching her, the other did the shopping. Irene told them about our tribulation, and how we suffered by not being able to acquire any food. After much telling, they promised to come whenever they could and help. Now that they knew where we resided, they would make sure that all other friends would come to help. Then they left, full of promises, and we had a feast.

Soon we had lots of visitors. All would bring whatever they could, and the best one was one called Elita. My dad helped him to acquire an excellent position in a company selling Elita soap, thus the name. Now he was president of the main coal depot in Lodz. He brought lots of provisions, including calf liver and plenty of onions. He loved the way my mom prepared it. We all ate the food, including Elita. Before he left, he made two promises—one, to send us all the coal we needed, and, two, that as long as he lived, he would not desert us.

True to his first promise, the next day a huge truck arrived loaded with the now priceless coal. Ours was the only tenement that didn't lack heat, at a time when even the Germans didn't get enough, for coal was strictly rationed. The building caretaker was overjoyed. We were sure that some of it found its way to the black market. He became our best friend.

For the next couple of weeks, we had many visitors. All brought something to help us with, including clothes confiscated from a funeral home, which we promptly gave to the janitor in exchange for little favors, mostly for keeping quiet. Much to our surprise, the brothers Auerbach showed up. They were now dressed in spotless German uniforms. Nevertheless, we were glad to see them. My parents inquired about their parents and were told that they now lived in the city (most likely in a Jewish home), and that they were very well off. No more farming for them.

Suddenly the visits stopped. The Germans began to patrol the streets. Fraternizing with Jews was punishable by death. Elita was the last one that dared to come; then even he stopped.

Then one day the Nazis ordered all Jews to leave the city. We were to move to a part of the city known as Baluty. It was the most primitive section of Lodz; no running water or sewers. They would establish a Jewish ghetto there.

6

The janitor, trying to be helpful, introduced my father to a Polish man who owned a building there, but he had to vacate it in order to make room for Jews. The man was willing to swap apartments. At first my parents hesitated, not sure if they wanted to make that move (as if we had a choice), but things had a way of deciding for us.

That same night, we heard shouting, then shooting. Soon the super came carrying an old orthodox Jew. The man was bleeding profusely from a bullet wound. He put the poor man on our kitchen floor. My parents tried to stop the bleeding, but to no avail. That night the man died; unfortunately, without my parents finding out anything about him or his family.

That sad incident finally convinced them that it was time to make the move. By morning, we had gathered our belongings, bought a sled from a neighbor, loaded it with all our possessions, then we walked the streets. It was freezing cold and snowing.

We arrived at our destination late. The Polish man was glad to see us; for him, too, it was time to move. Ours was a much nicer place, so he was pleased. His was much smaller. It consisted of a single bedroom, a combination of living and dining room, and a very small kitchen. By then, we were much too tired to care. We were exhausted from pushing the sled, so without any complaints, we went to sleep, all five of us on the one bed. Once again Mom and Dad slept on the couch.

We woke early, ate the little food we brought with us, and went in search of our Aunt Ethel and her brood, which consisted of three girls and one boy. He was eighteen, and his name was also David. The three girls were my cousin Zosia, who was sixteen, and her sisters Ruzia, thirteen, and Pola, eleven. My aunt was the only sibling my mother had in Lodz, Poland. She and her sister were the only ones that left Russia after Stalin came to Power and started his purges.

My mom was very close to Aunt Ethel, and we were very fond of them. We had their new address but had no knowledge of the neighborhood. The only time my mom went to that part of the city was when the boys needed new shoes, only because she had a distant cousin who was a cobbler, who lived there. Zenek hated those excursions. He complained that the streets were too narrow for him.

After a time, we found the place, which was even smaller than ours. We were overjoyed to see them. My Aunt Ethel and Uncle Srulek were happy to see us. They worried about us a lot. Auntie apologized for not feeding us; they had barely enough food for their children. Besides, our uncle was ill with tuberculosis and needed to be fed often.

Sadly, we left the family that used to make a banquet whenever we got together. Upon entering our new home, Mom began to cry; she felt bad for my aunt and uncle. When she calmed down, she realized that her own cupboards were empty. She asked our father to go out and try to buy some food. It took Dad almost an hour to find a store where he had to barter his gold watch for a small loaf of bread.

After that miserly lunch, I went out to look over our new surroundings. I met a girl my own age. At first she was shy and tried to hide, but after a while she overcame it, and we talked about everything. From her, I learned that there was a school open not far from my new home.

The girl's name was Kasia. We played hopscotch until it got dark. I asked her in for dinner, not realizing that we wouldn't have any. Upon finding that we had no food, Kasia asked Mom if she had any money. She said that she knew where to get groceries. Mom gave her the cash and told her to get anything she could. To us it didn't matter, since we had nothing at all.

We waited for her return. The apartment was cold, and we were very, very hungry. Yet no one complained. The boys lay on the sofa, Irene read a book, Mom was mending the boys' socks, and Dad was pacing the floor. I was nervous, unable to do or say anything. I was beginning to regret asking the girl, thinking that perhaps she took the money and never meant to return. In silence, we watched the clock ticking away. Outside, it got dark. Finally, Mom told us to prepare for bed, it was no use waiting. Suddenly, we heard footsteps, then a knock on the door. To my delight, in marched Kasia carrying a bag full of groceries. We gathered around the kitchen table, as mom prepared a feast. Never before did black bread and Polish kielbasa taste so good. Mom invited Kasia to partake, but she declined, saying that it was late and she had to go home, her grandma would worry. We thanked her profoundly, and I made her promise to return the next day.

That morning, I waited and waited, but Kasia did not come. I went outside searching, but she was nowhere in sight. Disappointed, I was about to give up, when a teenage girl approached me. She told me that Kasia had left. She and her grandmother had left for good. Besides, it was for the best. The girl explained that Kasia's mother was in jail for killing Kasia's father. Therefore, she was being raised by her grandma. I ran home and repeated what I was told to my mom, whereupon Mother told me that I should not think less of her. She was a sweet and good child, and if ever I saw her again, I should be a good friend to her for it was not her fault. Surely her father had deserved what her mother did to him, but the Poles being good Catholics had no qualms to put her mother away for life thus making the child an orphan for life.

Later that day, we went to see my aunt and cousins again. Mom took some of the food; she knew that they had none. I played with Ruzia and Pola. We could not help but listen to the grown-ups as they talked about the rest of our immediate family, and they expressed hope that my dad's brothers were safe. Besides Uncle Ruven, the one that went to the farm with his two sons and two daughters, my dad had another brother, Bernard, who was the black sheep in the family. He was an artist and owned a theater, where he and his two girls performed. He had no sons. He also was an editor and worked for the most anti-Semitic newspaper in Poland. If truth must be told, he was a sot who loved his whiskey. We children adored him and his wife and loved to visit with them. There were always famous actors in his home. I loved it when they would give me pictures, which they signed for me.

Once he convinced my parents to let me attend a ballet school run by the owners of the paper. I loved it and would have continued attending it, if it was not for a show that we performed. I was extremely proud of my part. It was a Christmas play, and I was Mary, the mother of Christ. My parents were invited. Dad seemed to enjoy it, but not so mother; she pulled me out pronto. My uncle Ruven heard about the fiasco and proclaimed, "I told you so." Well, that was the end of my career as a ballerina, but not my love for my favorite uncle.

Still, we were allowed to visit, even sleep over. We loved being there. Uncle Bernard would let us sneak into the theater and watch films that otherwise we would not be permitted to see.

Our favorite uncle fled Poland as soon as the Germans entered. He invented a piece of paper, which had a likeness of Hitler. When folded in a certain way, it became a pig and therefore a very popular joke among Jews and Poles alike. They left for Russia, and as far as we knew, never made it. The rest is in the annals of history.

7

Next, the Germans installed barbed wire all around the Ghetto and officially closed us in. The Ghetto was now left without any means of acquiring provisions. Stores closed for lack of merchandise.

Now the dreaded hunger began in a full force. It was sad to witness youngsters wandering the streets crying out loud, "I'm hungry!" As much as I, too, felt the hunger pains (yes, it hurts), I could not abide watching them, especially my own siblings—especially David and Zenek. I was glad to leave the house whenever I could. I enrolled in school, such as it was. It kept me away for a couple of hours. Then one day they closed it; it was forbidden for Jewish children to get an education. No more did I have a place to hide from the sadness I witnessed at my own home.

I began to spend my time outside, where at times it was even warmer than indoors, especially when the sun was out. Once, while sitting idle on the curb, deep in thought, I didn't realize that every one gone home, leaving the street deserted. Suddenly I heard the clatter of hoofs. I had no time to run. I sat there mesmerized. I saw a German astride a horse. Scared, I looked up at the man, expecting the worst.

Then I heard the man speak, calling me by my name. I looked up, and recognized him. He in turn jumped down, picked me up, and asked me to take him to my parents. That German was also a friend and a cousin of Erwin. I knew him well. Many a Christmas Eve we spent together at Erwin's home. He was also a boyfriend of my sister's best friend, but because the girl was Polish and not German, his family didn't approve of her. The lovers used to meet in our home, and at times Dad would lend him money so he could take the girl out. We entered our humble and freezing flat. He embraced Mom. He realized at once that she was suffering from malnutrition and a little dementia.

Foniek was his given name, but we called him Foik. He berated Dad for letting Mom get that way (as if it was Father's fault). Foik was now a big shot in the criminal police force located in the Ghetto. His job was to seek out rich Jews and beat them to a pulp in order to get what they still had. If the poor soul had nothing, the police would dispose of such a person the only way they knew, by shooting them. We heard about that place, but not about the man who was responsible for committing those vile deeds.

Before the war, Irene was told by her friend that Foik was beating up Jewish students. When she told Dad about it, he forbade her to repeat such "nonsense." Foik danced around holding Mom in his arms. He even gave me a pony ride on his back and acted as if nothing unusual had happened. Before he left, he promised to help us with food and medication for Mom. He would speak to a doctor and find out what she needed in order to get well.

After he left, Dad was in a daze. He could not accept that it was Foik, and that now he was the most cruel and horrific Nazi. Nevertheless, he allowed Irene to go to Foik, not so much for the food, but for the medicine Mom needed so badly. Irene came back loaded with groceries, vitamins, and vials of a miracle drug, which would give Mom a new lease on life. Dad didn't waste any time: he found a doctor who would give Mom the injections.

At first, she did quite well. We were surprised how quickly she recuperated. She began to clean and cook again. We were happy to see her doing so well. Again, we would visit her beloved sister. We shared some of the food with her and her family, and life didn't look so dismal.

Irene knitted little sweaters for Foik's baby (he now had one) and for her friend who he was now married to. Irene went often to see him, and true to his promise, he continued to help us. Foik even gave us some seeds to grow vegetables. We turned the backyard into a little miniature farm where we grew cabbage, carrots, green beans, and cucumbers.

I learned that life is not constant. People began to suspect that Irene was working for the police as an informer. She refused to continue meeting Foik. When she didn't come to see him, he came to us. Dad explained why, and that it was better that way. Foik suggested that instead of coming inside that place, he would arrange for her to go and see the police station's gardener. He ordered the man to supply all that we needed.

The gardener was a distant cousin of my dad's. He even had the same last name as we. He was not happy about helping us. He had some silly grudge against Dad, and he took it out on poor Irene. She refused to go to him, for he made her feel like a beggar. Instead, she decided to wait early each morning for Foik across the street.

Mom began to slip again. Dad could not understand why. One day, while the doctor was visiting, Dad left the apartment to see a neighbor. Upon returning, he looked through the window and spotted the doctor filling the syringe with water. When dad accused him, the doctor began to cry and admitted that he had been doing it for some time. He wanted the medication for his own wife, who also suffered from malnutrition. Dad forgave the doctor, but from then on he made sure to watch when he administered to Mom.

In meanwhile, all around us the circumstances were becoming unbearable. More and more people were dying of hunger. My Uncle Srulek was one of them. This was a blow for me. He was the first in our family to die, and we all took it very hard, especially my aunt and cousins.

For some reason unknown to me, Foik stopped helping us. No more food or medicine. It's possible that he, too, was threatened by the SS. Irene stopped meeting with him, so once again we had no food or medicine for Mother, and no coal or wood to heat what little space we had. Dad bartered the little jewelry he still had for a kilo of potato peels, which we cooked and ate, but even this was hard to get.

People were walking around like zombies, crying "Jestem glodny" (I'm hungry!) and collapsing on the street. There was nothing anyone could do about it. We had nothing to give them. The cold was unbearable. The walls inside our apartment were glistening like diamonds from condensation. Even in bed, we didn't have enough blankets to keep warm.

Dad tried hard to provide what little food he could buy, beg for, or steal, but to no avail. Then one day, accidentally, he came across a former partner of his, who was doing quite well for himself and his family, which consisted of his wife and his two little girls. The man had a job at the main depot, where he worked unloading trucks of the little food the Ghetto was now receiving. Consequently, he was able to steal some of it. Thus his family fared well. In desperation, Dad had asked him if there was a possibility that they could share some of it with his youngest girl, me. Mathias suggested that I should come to his apartment at five o'clock when his wife fed the children, then I too would be fed. Upon arriving home, Dad excitedly explained to me that at least one of us would get some decent food. Since I knew that family well, I had no qualms about it. I merrily skipped all the way to the place where I would get something to eat. His wife greeted me warmly, she sat me down next to the girls. The older one was seven years old and the baby was two. She explained that I would have to wait while she fed her children, and when they had had their fill, whatever was left over I would get. I did not care, especially when I smelled the beautiful aroma of chicken soup. Luckily for me, they left some of it, which she gave me.

Three days in a row I ate the leftovers. On the fourth day when I arrived, she told me that the baby was ill and refused to eat, but if I could help out and feed the little one then I, too, would be fed. I did my best and got some of the soup into her. Suddenly, she began to vomit and most of it went right into the bowl. The mother picked her up, calmed her down and cleaned the child and added that it was not my fault for the baby was sick. Then she took the bowl put it in front of me saying "Eat, eat. It's good for you." I was abhorred. As hungry as I was, I could not eat it. I ran crying all the way home and told my Dad that I would rather die of hunger than eat that soup. And that was the last day I went there.

The tenement was now being torn apart for wood, including the outhouse, whose doors were taken out. We had to go in pairs in order to relieve ourselves. One would stay in front, holding up a blanket; thus, we preserved a little bit of privacy.

I stopped reading children's stories and perused anything I could lay my hands on. I daydreamed of a normal life, like the heroines in the books. I longed for it with all my heart. At times, I remembered the wonderful life I led, the friends I had, and wondered why, what did we do? Were we bad people? When I asked my dad about it, he would say, No. It was only because we were Jews. "But we are no different from others," I would say. Then my father would look away, for he had no plausible answer.

Then one day our staircase disappeared. We had to climb through the window—very scary. Luckily for us, Dad was able to find a new dwelling around the corner. It was in a little house with only four apartments. Two stood empty; the previous tenants succumbed to hunger or cold, I'm not sure. All we knew was that the rooms on the first level became available that same day.

We moved in in a hurry, afraid that someone else would beat us to it. It consisted of one large room that we divided into two by placing the furniture a certain way. Someone found out that there was petrified wood in the ground. We began to dig and sift through the dirt like gold prospectors of old. It took the whole family hours to fill a bucket enough to light a fire for a short time, and if we were lucky enough, we would sell some for a piece of bread to make the so-called bread soup for all of us. Somehow we survived, despite the hardships.

8

The ghetto was beginning to take shape, thanks to the Gmina, a Jewish agency, which tried to do the best it could under the circumstances. Most of the population was from Lodz and surrounding villages. We even had a president, an elderly man, whose name was Haim Rumkowsky. Before the war, he was the director of an orphanage. The story that was told went something like this. When the Germans first entered the Gmina, they inquired, "Who is the oldest here?" Rumkowsky stepped forward, for he was the senior of that group. That was the way he was chosen, and he became president.

Miracle of miracles. The Germans sent in wagons of potatoes. The president was not sure how to distribute the trove. While he considered that dilemma, the weather turned even colder, the much desired tubers froze and became unfit for human consumption. Rumkowsky ordered his henchmen to spray them with gasoline. The hungry masses became angry and stormed the warehouse. They took the now poisonous potatoes and ate them. Soon dysentery broke out; most of them died. The ghetto became decimated.

Some food was now coming into the ghetto. This time the Gmina opened soup kitchens. We had to wait in line for hours for that miserly watery prize. A whole new enterprise began to emerge, smuggling. One had to take off the Star of David, which we had to wear instead of the armband, cross the barbed wire, and venture into the forbidden land of plenty.

Irene was one of the first to do it. Somehow, she learned that a couple she knew owned a grocery store not too far from the ghetto. Irene became the breadwinner in the family. Whatever we could afford we kept; the rest we sold on the now-thriving black market.

For a few weeks we fared well, then the axe fell. Irene was found out, most likely reported by Poles. She was arrested and beaten so badly that she was unable to stand. She was released to the Jewish police. They brought her home on a stretcher, her back scarred for life. It broke my heart to see her suffer. This once strong beautiful girl lay in bed unable to move. Both my parents administered to her day and night.

The food she once so selflessly supplied and paid so dearly for was no longer being provided. That's when I decided to take over. My parents would not agree, but I conspired with David to do so. It was easy for me for I didn't "look Jewish at all." David would help me cross the barbed wire after stealing the money needed for shopping from my parents.

I started my career enthusiastically and became the youngest smuggler in the ghetto. Walking the streets of "Freedomland," fear took hold of me. What if I too were to be arrested? I started to hum a well-known childhood song in order to give myself courage. Then I heard a commotion. Directly across the street, I witnessed an arrest. A couple of Jewish teenage girls were being taunted by Polish youths, who chanted "Jews, Jews." Then the police made the arrest. Since there was nothing I could do about it I continued on my way, all the time laughing as if it was amusing and I, too, was Polish.

Finally, I found the store. David knew that it was the one Irene used, and he made sure that I, too, would go there. I entered, not knowing what to expect. To my relief, it was empty. Somehow, the owners knew who I was. They greeted me like a long-lost friend, which put me at ease. Mr. Miller took me into their kitchen. He sat me down at the table and put a plate of food in front of me. I devoured it not unlike a hungry dog, and I felt shame for doing it. Then Mrs. Miller came in, and she began to question me. She asked about Irene. She must have suspected that something bad had befallen her. I told her what happened, and that from now on I would come. Both of them sympathized, even shed tears, and I felt that I was safe with them. Mrs. Miller packed a whole bag of groceries. She must have known what I needed, for she didn't ask. She did tell me what was in the bag. I paid and started for home.

For me, the trek home was easy. No one bothered me. I approached the designated spot where I would cross back. David was there waiting. He stretched the wire, and I was back inside the ghetto. Once there, I began to shake uncontrollably. David pretended that he didn't see it. I did not say anything about the incident I witnessed for fear that he would not allow me to go again.

Once I entered the apartment carrying the bag of groceries, my parents realized what David and I were doing, but because we needed it so very badly, they didn't scold us. I continued to do it every day. We now had the badly needed food and money. I was happy to be able to provide and to see Dad, Mom, and the boys having meals. Irene was still unable to get of bed, but thanks to me she now had something to eat.

Steve met a young girl; they fell madly in love. He spent most of his waking hours at her home. Zenek and David played all kinds of games again, while I sat thinking about my next trip and worrying what might happen to me if or when I got caught. It seemed like the whole ghetto was on the move, including my cousins Pola and Ruzia.

The Gestapo became wise to it. They proclaimed that anyone caught on the forbidden streets would be put to death. Then, in order to put a stop to smuggling, they placed armed police on every corner with orders to shoot the perpetrators. It became terribly hard to continue; yet, I was not willing to stop. Against my parent's advice, who feared for my life, I went on smuggling.

Directly across from the barbed wire, on the Polish side, there was a small grocery store. The owner of it was a typical Polish-German. We all feared him. He would stand in front of his business and watch. As someone would cross, he would immediately call the police. I would wait until he had a customer and went inside; I then ran as fast as I could. I thought and thought about it, then I formed a plan. I didn't tell any one about it, not even David. The next time I crossed over was when he was watching. Boldly I approached him and told him that I needed groceries. I asked if it would be all right by him, if I were able to do my shopping in his store. David, who watched the whole time, was shocked by my boldness and amazed when Mr. Shultz took me inside. I told him what I needed; he sold me all I asked for.

What a great relief it was for me; no more would I have to walk the dreaded streets. I continued to shop at Shultz's. Then somehow the Gestapo got wind of it. Shultz got scared and refused to do business with me. I was forced to go to the Millers again.

Once, on my way back, as I was reentering the ghetto, I heard shouting. "Stop!" David pulled me over, while bullets were flying all around us. We ran into a doorway and stood there shaking until it got quiet. Then we ran home. We didn't tell anyone about it, for fear that we would be forbidden to continue smuggling. Again and again I went out of the Ghetto, until once, as I was turning the corner, I was approached by two policemen, one Polish and one German. They asked for papers. Since I didn't have any, I made believe that I didn't understand them. A Polish woman came over and tried to help me. She told them that she knew me; that I was her neighbor's child, even though she knew that I was from the ghetto. That showed me that there were some nice Poles.

Even now, I don't know what possessed me. Maybe it was stupidity or pride. I refused her help and told them that indeed I was a Jew. I was arrested and taken to the nearest precinct, where I was questioned and made to wait for someone to take me to the Baluter Mark, the place where Irene was so badly maimed. Outside, it started to rain. I sat waiting, full of terrible fear. Then I heard the officer in charge asking for a cigarette. None of the policemen had any. I knew that I had a whole carton and bravely I told him so. To my astonishment, he accepted only one, when I would have been willing to give him all.

A short time later, the same officer announced that he was ready to go home. Since my destination was on his way, he would take me there. The rain let up a little. As we started on our way, we walked close to the wires that surrounded the ghetto. Suddenly it began to pour. We came close to a watch house, where he decided to take shelter. The soldier asked him why he ventured outside in that horrible weather. He explained that he had a Jewess under arrest, and he had to take me to the Baluter Mark. "Man, you must be crazy," the soldier said, "in this lousy rain to walk a mile. Why don't you just let her go back into that hell on earth? I will turn my back and you let her get inside." I could not believe what I heard. Could it be a ploy? Will he shoot me? Scared as I was, I could not do anything but obey. The officer took me to the fence and ordered me to cross. My hands were shaking badly. I fumbled with the wire and could not stretch it enough. Then the officer helped, and in the act of trying to cross, I completely forgot my precious bundle. To my surprise, he handed me the parcel.

Once inside, fear took hold of me. I shook like a leaf. My teeth were chattering uncontrollably. I ran like I was amok. My family could not believe that I came back in one piece. David, who witnessed the arrest, told my parents, who once again expected their child on a stretcher or worse, maybe even dead. Overjoyed to have me back, they made me swear that never again would I cross over the barbed wire.

It took us only a couple of weeks to use up the last of the provisions. Again we were at the mercy of the Gmina. We did get ration card but no rations. The only food we got was, again, the watery soup, except that now it was cabbage spiced with cabbage worms. For this delicacy we had to stay in line. Often, by the time we came to the window, we were told that there was no more.

One day, after standing in line the whole afternoon, David came home half frozen and announced that he couldn't take any more. The Germans were asking for volunteers, and he was ready to leave for Germany. There was nothing my parents could do to persuade him otherwise. We only hoped that possibly, while working for the Nazis, he might get the food that a growing young man needed. Steve, too, decided to go. Before they left, Steve gave Helen his ring. Both families agreed and called it an engagement.

Two days later, they and about a hundred others left, destination unknown. The apartment seemed empty. We all were sad, especially Mom. I could hear her crying at night. From that time on her mind faltered more and more. She would complain about the quantity and/or the quality of the rations, if and when we got any. She refused to prepare them, saying that horsemeat was not what she liked to cook. This great lady who had previously entertained lavishly could not accept the harsh reality of ghetto life. It hurt me more to watch her dissipate than the hunger and cold hurt me.

It saddened me to watch Zenek. He was so close to David. Now he became so very quiet. Irene tried hard to explain to him that David would be better off away from the Ghetto. She was beginning to recuperate and began to take over the chores from Mom. After the boys left, Dad became a beaten man, a shadow of himself

9

1941. That year started a little calmer. Under Rumkowsky, with the cooperation of one German named Bibof, factories opened. In order to receive rations plus soup, all had to go to work. No work, no food. The rations consisted of 250 grams of bread and some vegetables: mostly beets, carrots and big white radishes, which we soaked overnight and squeezed them in order to get the bitterness out.

Haim Rumkowsky held a speech and announced that in a year or two, the ghetto would run like a well-oiled machine. Everyone thought that he had lost his mind. Even under the better circumstances, we didn't expect to last that long. As if the Ghetto weren't crowded enough, the Nazis brought transports of Jews from Germany, Austria and all the little shtetles (towns) in Poland.

We were ordered to share our living quarters with strangers. We were assigned a young couple from Vienna, Kurt and Edith. They were arrested while honeymooning. Kurt wasn't Jewish, so he didn't have to go, but he opted to stay with his beloved bride. They were told that they were being resettled to a nice city—no mention of a ghetto.

We liked having them. Father especially liked Kurt. The two of them schemed to let Kurt's family know their whereabouts. At that time, we were corresponding with Steve and David. Their letters were not what we had hoped for. They were being worked to death for a little miserly food, and treated as no more than slaves.

Hoping that they received our replies, Dad devised a plan. Knowing that the mail was censured, he wrote that Cousin Kurt and his wife were visiting us in Lodz. He gave them the address of Kurt's family in Vienna. It worked. Soon we got a letter stating that they were corresponding with them, even receiving food packages in return.

As unexpected as the arrival of the young pair was, that was how fast they left. The Germans apologized to the Vienna Jews, telling them that it was a mistake. They didn't have to stay in the Lodz ghetto; the Austrian Jews could go back home. Not realizing that it was a sham, the young couple was overjoyed. We were sorry to see them leave. Edith left all her clothes for Irene, saying that she had plenty at her home. The next morning they left, and we never heard from them again.

As soon as that dismal episode ended, a great misfortune befell us, one we had all dreaded. The Nazis declared that children were a hindrance to the working parents; thus, they would move them to a nice orphanage outside the ghetto, where the youngsters would be properly cared for. Somehow, no one believed them.

The distraught parents refused to give up their children. Haim Rumkowsky informed the people that the order must be obeyed, or the whole Ghetto population would pay the consequences for disobeying, and pay dearly. Still, no one listened. The Jewish police were ordered to forcefully round up the tots and deliver them to the Nazis. They were met with an onslaught of furious parents and were unable to perform that abhorrent task.

The Germans retaliated by conducting a house-by-house search. Some parents, expecting the worse, hid their offspring in hideous places, including outhouses, or buried them in ditches, even in water holes. Still, most children were taken by cruel force.

Prior to that horrendous order, Foik sent a message to Dad advising him to hide Zenek and me. He disclosed that the Nazis were sending a special division known as the "Uberfallkommando." He explained that he preferred not to be a witness to that carnage.

Dad and Irene worked that whole night. They dug a hole under the kitchen floor for Zenek and me. We were to hide there as soon as we heard the Nazis coming. Early that morning, while we ate our miserly breakfast, all hell broke loose. We heard dogs barking and shouts, "Out, out."

Dad tried to make the two of us hide under the floor, but I got frightened and refused to do it. Zenek was the only one to listen to Dad. We were ordered to line up in front of our building. A Nazi pointed me toward the waiting truck. Then, when he turned toward his next victim, Dad pushed me into a doorway, whispering, "Hide." I remember entering an empty room. The rest is blank.

Later, I was told that I was found crumbled on the floor behind a heavy curtain, but there was no rejoicing. In that terrible confusion, while Dad was occupied watching me, he lost track of Mother, who at that split second attacked a Nazi who was trying to pull an infant out of its mother's arms. Mother clawed at the German's face. She was then dragged into a waiting truck and taken away. For the rest of my life, I will regret that I didn't listen to father. If it had not been for my fit of terror, maybe Mother would have been safe. I still can't erase the guilt I feel even today.

Mindless of the risk and hoping that perhaps Foik would be in, Irene ran to find him. Unfortunately the Kripo was closed. Brokenhearted, she made her way back through the now deserted streets, crying bitterly, only to be faced by Aunt Ethel. Bad news travels fast. She was told by someone who witnessed the whole tragedy. Aunt Ethel was hysterical; she even accused Dad of allowing the Nazis to take her beloved sister. After she left, Dad lay down. I thought that he felt guilty and could not face us, even though it was my fault. That night I heard my dad cry bitterly.

Zenek was behaving strangely. He was talking to someone. We realized that he was having a conversation with our mother. At that time, we didn't know anything about nervous breakdowns. Much later, a doctor explained to Father what it was. We kept quiet and made believe that Mom was there.

No one went to work anymore. The Nazis were still on the rampage, grabbing children and anybody they wanted. They emptied the hospitals by throwing infants from windows onto waiting trucks below.

The next day, a tearful Zosia showed up. She told us that Aunt Ethel and her two younger sisters were among the many that were taken that day. Zosia said that she begged them to let her go also, but the sadistic Nazis would not let her. They took pleasure in breaking families apart. Dad prevailed upon her to stay with us as part of our immediate family.

After that bloody week, the chairman announced that the remaining population was now safe, providing we go back to work. As long as we produce the goods the Reich needed, they would leave us alone.

I worked in a factory where we made shoes from rags. Nothing was being wasted. The shoes were for the Wehrmacht that fought on the Russian front. I missed Mom terribly and felt forlorn. At work, I was not allowed to think, but once home I sobbed myself to sleep until I had no more tears to shed. After all those years, I'm still hesitant to open the wounds inflicted upon us, and the cruel way we lost Mother.

That year, we were constantly beset by horrendous afflictions. Infested with lice, we spent hours like apes, delousing one another, with little success. Next the dreaded typhus came and spread like a wild fire. There was hardly a household that was not touched by it, including ours. Irene was the one that came down with it. We all were quarantined for the duration of her illness. Now my much-loved sister was deathly sick. We feared for her life. We had no medication and no hope that she would survive. There was absolutely nothing we could do but watch her as her condition deteriorated. With what little food we had, we tried to feed her, but she could not swallow any of it. As afraid as we were of catching it from her, we didn't let the food be wasted. We ate her leftovers. By staying home, we were deprived of the soup we would get at the factory, and we were starving more then ever. It was depressing to watch the death wagons collecting the young corpses from every building.

Meanwhile, we looked on helplessly as Irene grew weaker with each passing day. By some miracle, our father found a physician who declared that he would try to help her by using the same method he used on the soldiers during the First World War. We had nothing to lose and allowed him to dip her in ice-cold water, alternating with hot water (we used the kitchen table as firewood in the stove). Thus he was able to break the high temperature that was eating her alive. The doctor did cure her of typhus, but at the same time she had gotten many other complications. Fortunately, she survived, when so many died.

After her bout of illness, Irene was too weak to walk to work by herself. I never forgot how this strong-willed girl had to lean on me while walking. I had to get up each morning at four o'clock to get her ready, then take her to her factory. Afterwards, I went to my plant. I didn't mind it for I was happy that she had made it. I learned that as long as there is life, there is hope.

10

The typhus was slowly disappearing; fewer and fewer people were contracting it. Life went on as than before. Now the lucky ones who had made it displayed a defiance.

During those bleak years, my dad found time not only for us, his children, but also for many youngsters. It seemed that they found solace by just being near him. He gave them courage and implored them not to despair but to think of the future. He would put on shows and make them sing, and convinced them that they would make it. Above all else, he gave them hope.

Every Sunday, they gathered in our home—boys and girls, Irene's and Zosia's friends. Those degraded teens got uplifted spirits by just being near Dad. They flirted, and love was still a part of everyone's dreams. Some even married and begat children. Haim Rumkowsky himself performed the wedding ceremonies. I had a terrible crush on one young man who frequently came to the gatherings. I used to wait breathlessly for his visits; I even daydreamed about him at work. I must have been influenced by the many romantic novels I had read. Unfortunately, the love of my life didn't even know that I existed. He was enamored with a pretty and extremely talented girl. I didn't stand a chance. He didn't show up for a couple of weeks, and I just new that something terrible had befallen him. Then we were told that he had contracted the typhus and succumbed to it. I was devastated. For a while I mourned, but that was a fact of life in the ghetto—here today and gone tomorrow. Soon I was preoccupied with new things.

Irene had gotten a new job. The Germans opened a new factory. Because they were making appliqués from real gold and silver for the officer's uniforms, they didn't trust Jews. It was a plant that employed German civilians only, with the exception of Irene. She was highly recommended, most likely by Foik. Dad became caretaker of our building. He liked being home; it gave him time to make sure that we had a little something when we came home from work.

I was transferred to a dress factory, where I was taught to operate a sewing machine (a manual one). My job consisted of putting sleeves on garments. After a short time, the management opened a school, which I attended. We were taught how to make patterns for dresses and also the three R's. Of course, it was forbidden to educate Jewish children, but somehow it was done. I was the youngest one there, and the teachers gave me a lot of special attention.

Zenek worked in a leather-tanning factory. He was still confused and often spoke to Mother. It made me mad and very sad when his co-workers called him crazy.

Zosia worked in a place where they made plastic raincoats. It was a dangerous job. After a while, the workers would contract tuberculosis. Dad worried about her a lot. He convinced Irene to ask her boss to employ Zosia there. Irene was waiting for the right time, and as luck would have it, it came. She saved a German girl's life. When the stupid girl let her hair get caught in the machine she was operating, Irene had the presence of mind to shut off the main electric switch. As a reward, they made her a director, and she was given a special ration card called "bairut," which was only given to the president's advisers and his henchmen. Irene officially changed Zosia's last name to ours. Then she asked her boss if she could take her sister in; thus, Zosia got a job at Irene's factory.

We relaxed for a while, thinking that all was well, but it was not to be. With the cooperation of Rumkowsky, the Nazis began to resettle those whose family members had "volunteered" for work in Germany.

As always, the Germans were resourceful in killing two birds with one stone. They proclaimed that all those whose children or siblings worked in Germany were to be deported to a much better camp. This time, we were wise to their promises. We realized that it was a ploy to get rid of those whose children or siblings were in Germany and the family received a miserly nine marks monthly per worker. Once they got rid of those whose children or siblings worked in Germany, they wouldn't have to shell out the money.

Our president decided that first to go would be the single survivors. Luckily, we had changed Zosia's last name to ours. It was just in time; otherwise, she would have been deported, since her brother David was also working in Germany. Once they were done with the singles, the Jewish police began to round up the rest of the recipients. The police did their dirty work well.

We, too, were taken for "resettlement." At the police station, Dad prevailed upon the officer in charge to allow Irene go out to see Foik. The officer humored dad and agreed, not expecting results. He allowed her one hour. We waited her return on pins and needles, wondering if she would be able to see Foik. Within the allotted time, Irene returned. She told everyone that Foik promised that he'd see to everything and not to worry. She came loaded with all kinds of goodies, including a bottle of vodka. A short time later Rumkowky himself arrived, ordering our release. It was said that he was threatened by our "friend" that the whole ghetto would be burned if even one hair on our heads was harmed. Father decided to celebrate our release right there at the precinct. The police, amazed, joined in, partaking in the festivity. They even apologized for arresting our family.

Once at home, it dawned on me that, if not for Foik, we would have been on our way to God knows where, and possibly we were saved from a great danger. The news of our escape from deportation spread quickly, and great speculation ensued as to what really happened to the ones sent out from the ghetto, for they were never heard of again.

Afterwards, we were sought out by the big shots, for they, too, were not safe from "resettlement" or arrests by the dreaded criminal police. They would often beg Irene to intervene when they were taken by the Kripo. Quite a few were saved by Irene, especially the ones that had children.

Once Helen had the "pleasure" of meeting Foik and his henchmen who came looking for her father, as he had a brother in the United States. They knew that the family had visas for America, which the Nazis didn't recognize, and they assumed that he had gold or dollars, which he was hiding. Those possessions were punishable by death if not given to the Nazis. While the murderers were making havoc, Foik spotted a portrait of Steve hanging on the wall. He asked the now petrified Helen why was there a likeness of Steve there. She explained that he was her fiancé. Foik immediately ordered his men to put everything back in place and to leave them be. Right after they left, she came to tell us what took place at her home and how her dad was saved by Steve's portrait.

Irene announced that she was getting married. She met the man at the time we were detained at the police station. He, too, was a police officer. He was an extremely handsome young man and highly educated. A German Jew, he and his family came to Poland at the time Hitler came to power. While interned in the ghetto, his parents took ill, and both of them passed away. Irene and he were seeing each other for some time; now they decided to get married.

Dad was pleased, and so were Zosia and Zenek, but I was sad. For me, it meant that she would leave our home and go to live with him, far away from us. I felt as if I were losing my mom all over again. I was afraid to express my thoughts—afraid that I would mar her happiness. Zosia was the only one that felt my unhappiness. She sensed my need for a sister or mother.

She assured me that she would be close to me, just as Irene had been. Every day, she would tell me about the work they performed, and how much the masters liked Irene and her. She liked being with me, and we proved to be as close as two sisters could be.

I continued working and learning at the plant. By then, I even sewed dresses. At night I would study and read anything I could lay my hands on. It was a kind of escape from the misery we had to endure. I became addicted to books. It helped me to escape from the ghetto and the pangs of hunger that continued to plague us.

No matter how hard we tried, we still had to contend with the infestation of lice, even though we were given a small bar of soap to cleanse ourselves with. Not until the war ended did we know that this soap was made from human fat—Jewish fat. Each bar had the initisls RJS, which stood for "Rein Juden Seife" (pure Jewish soap).

11

Dad was a very special man, respected an loved by all who knew him, Orthodox Jews and unbelievers alike. The very religious called his a "Tzadik," a righteous person, a man of good deeds. I remember a special incident, because it involved me personally. I came into the Ghetto with two pairs of shoes: one which I wore everyday, and the other pair I kept for special occasions. The day in question I came across my friend Ada. I had not seen my friends since the war began. Ada told me that she was in touch with some of them, especially Halinka and Sarenka. Now she would invite them that Sunday, and we would have a reunion. I was elated and looked forward to seeing my friends. Upon arriving home, the first thing I did was look for my precious shoes. I panicked for I could not find them.

Seeing how distraught I was, Zenek revealed that Dad gave them to a little girl from the orphanage. I could not understand why. Why my beloved father would do such a vile thing to me. When Dad came in, I asked if it was true; he confirmed it. I became enraged. I sobbed and I screamed for a long time. Nothing he said appeased me. I insisted that he had no right to give away the only good pair of shoes I possessed to a perfect stranger. Instead of being mad at me, he took me in his arms, explaining that he watched that little barefoot waif walking to work in all kinds of weather. He could not bear it any longer, and he decided to do what was right for that child. She was an orphan and had no one to care for her, while I had him to watch over me, and he would see to it that I never had to go barefoot. The following week, he presented me with a pair of sandals that he himself fashioned. The soles were wooden; for the straps he used the handles of our mattress. I must admit that they were really pretty and fit me perfectly. He was right. I had him to take care of my needs.

Then one dreadful day, the SS Kommandos came again looking for the little ones they missed previously. Just as before, the Nazis made us line up in front of the building. We stood there while they searched each house. We knew that our neighbor, Mrs. Birenbaum, and her three-year-old child were hiding in the attic. When the Nazis were about to enter the building, Dad stepped forward and in his perfect German, assured the officer in charge that it would be a waste of time to do so. There were no more children in that house. The officer looked closely at Dad and replied, "Dancing teacher (he must have known him), you better be telling the truth or I will personally shoot you." Then he ordered his men to proceed to the next building. My father became the hero of the whole neighborhood. Dad saved the child to live another day.

The mother, Mrs. Birenbaum, was legally blind. She was maimed by her own husband, who, as a result of his crazy jealousy, threw acid in her face. At that time she was pregnant with his child. He himself committed suicide.

Little Sevek was born just before the war. Mrs. Birenbaum moved into the ghetto with her elderly father and the baby. Her dad died shortly after. All who knew that child adored him, especially my dad. He spent hours teaching him about a different world, one where people were free and good and were able to travel to faraway lands. Often Sevek asked Dad, "How big is this world? Is it much bigger than the ghetto? Is there a barbed-wire fence around it?"

This little boy was a clever little imp. For instance, while his mother stood in line for bread, Sevek would show up twirling a dead mouse on a string, thus scaring away the standing at the head of the line, so his mother would not have to wait in the cold so long. We had nicknamed him Tarzan because in all kinds of weather he would walk about in nothing but his underpants.

Then there was the time when Irene received an apple from a German co-worker. This gem presented a dilemma. What to do with it: should we barter it for bread, or for soup? Dad spoke up. He suggested we introduce little Sevek to it; he never saw one, much less tasted one. As usual, Dad had the last word. Not unlike King Solomon, he proclaimed that the little tot should know what an apple looked like and, what's more, the way it tasted. Sadly, we all parted with the apple. Our hope of getting some food for it disappeared once Dad had made a decision.

I feel this child was truly a precious little boy and I will mourn him for the rest of my life.

12

We lived peacefully a few more months, always dreading what was to come. There were constantly rumors of new troubles. We heard that people from the small villages were exterminated, or as the Nazis were fond of saying, "relocated." In order to quash those rumors, President Rumkowsky was taken to the Warsaw Ghetto, where the Germans put on a good show. They presented Rumkowsky with a well-running place. The president was convinced that by working full speed and respecting the German laws, we, too, would be left alone. No more resettlements. He was impressed with the way the Warsaw Ghetto was treated.

The weather was nice, and I enjoyed working with other youngsters. I made friends with most of them. The plant was on the other side of the bridge, which the Germans had the men of the ghetto build. It was a wooden structure. The two sides were separated by rails, where a streetcar ran for Poles and Germans; thus, both sides of the Ghetto were reunited by that bridge. Looking down at those streecars I often wondered what those free people thought about those people caged-in like animals. They could not avoid seeing us and the way we looked. We were walking "klapsedras" (which meant a public obituary) the walking dead. Sarcastically, we used to describe each other that way.

Since I had no formal Jewish education because my family was very assimilated, Helen's mother decided to teach me about the history of my people. She also taught me to speak and write Jewish, Yiddish. She read stories from the bible about our benevolent God who watched over his children, and how he took the Jews out of Egypt. I was fascinated by those tales. I learned a lot from that lady.

On our street lived a young Talmudic student. He would wander the streets telling stories from the holy book. He was a little demented as a result of studying the Kabala. Once I asked him where was our God now that we needed him so much to which he replied that God, being a Jew, studied the Talmud constantly, even when he was relieving himself in the bathroom. And he was so preoccupied that he forgot his children.

Shortly after that interaction, it was the Jewish New Year (Rosh Hashana). The students at the factory decided to make a greeting card for our much-loved teacher. Because I lived close to her, I was chosen to deliver the card to her. On the way there, I came upon a great commotion: people running; crying. I asked one of them what had happened. I was told that some Orthodox Jews were praying in a cellar of an abandoned building, and praying was strictly forbidden. Suddenly the structure had collapsed killing them all. Right then and there, I lost my belief in the Creator . . . I decided to live my life the best way I could, do what I knew was right, and just follow in my dad's footstep and be a good person and never to rely on a supreme being. There were no miracles for us Jews. The only miracle was life itself—to cherish the time we had, even if it was harsh, and to hope that the world would soon destroy the evil people, and that possibly we would be rescued.

13

1944. The axe had fallen. The Nazis decided to liquidate the Ghetto and began to evacuate everyone. At first they emptied the hospital, then they closed the factories. We stayed home, bewildered, not knowing what would happen to us. Irene came to see us. She brought some food with her that she received from the Birut card. We needed it badly. Now that we were not getting that soup at the factory, we were even more hungry. She was the one that told us about the resettlement but didn't know how or when it would happen. A day later, they came for us. Zenek was not at home, he was out scavenging for some food. He went looking for a certain weed that was quite good when cooked.

The Nazis gave us time to pack some essentials, then we were taken by trucks to the station. Dad was devastated with worry about Zenek. Suddenly the convoy stopped. We heard shouting, then we saw two soldiers. Zenek was with them. He pointed to us and told them that this was his family. They allowed him to climb on the truck.

Zenek explained what happened. Upon arriving home, he found the place empty. He went out looking for us, then he met a neighbor who came out of hiding. He told Zenek that we were taken away only a short time ago. Zenek began to run and soon came across the convoy. He begged the soldiers to unite him with his family. With the Nazis' approval, he was brought to us. How humane of them!

Riding through the other side of the Ghetto, we saw empty houses, open windows, and clothes strewn about; it was an eerie feeling. Yet, after witnessing that carnage, we still believed that we would be taken to some other ghetto for work. After all, the Germans needed us for work and the goods we produced.

Upon arriving at the station, we each were given a loaf of black bread and a bottle of unrefined oil for the trip. It was much more than we were ever given. There were hundreds there. After some time, the Jewish police herded us like livestock into cattle trains. The wagons were filled above capacity, perhaps fifty or sixty people in one car. There was no room to stand, much less to sit on the wooden floor. The pushing and shoving was unbearable. There was no air to breathe, except for the lucky ones that stood near the tiny window. There was a waste bucket for the bodily functions and no water. That was all there was.

We heard a whistle, and the train began to move. We were on our way, destination unknown. Lack of air made me choke, and I began to gasp and wheeze. Dad prevailed upon a man who stood next to the little window to hoist me up for a breath of fresh air. Watching most of the youngsters gasping for breath, Dad held a speech. He explained that now was the time to behave like civilized people. We must try to help each other and to make a little room for the children so they would have a place to sit or lie down. Dad's words had a calming effect on most of them. Unfortunately, there were some that didn't adhere. No sooner had I lay down than someone sat down on top of me. I screamed. Dad came to my rescue and pushed the woman off me.

Somehow, we made it through the night. The next morning, while the men took turns looking out the window in order to figure out where we were heading for. Dad held me up. We were passing a farm where there were some Poles working. While watching the train, they began to point toward us and began to laugh. They also made gestures as if cutting their throats. Very funny. I shall never forgive my countrymen for that cruel pantomime.

For breakfast, we ate a piece of the bread followed by a swallow of oil. We ate sparingly for fear that the trip would be a long one. Little Sevek begged his mother for a bit more. His mom refused, trying to explain to the child that he would need it later. The child began to wail. My dad broke off a piece of his bread and handed it to the boy. It upset me, and I told him so. He hushed me and said something that at that time I did not comprehend. Dad said, "Let the child have enough bread, for once in his short life."

As it turned out, the trip lasted only a few hours more, and when we arrived at the mysterious camp, we had a lot left over. We passed through a gate on which was a sign declaring, "Work will set you free." Then we heard a band playing a lively tune.

The train came to a stop. The doors opened to an unforgettable scene. Men in prison uniforms jumped in and began to throw our suitcases out. Then they shouted to the mothers to hand over their children to the elderly and sickly. The women refused to listen. The men tore the little ones out of the parents' arms and handed them over to the old women.

As soon as we disembarked, the men were separated from us women. Also, the elderly, the sick, and children were put to the left of us. There were trucks waiting for them. They were told that it was too far for them to walk.

Lucky for me, I was wearing Mother's shoes, which had high heels. Thus I appeared tall and was allowed to join the young women. Next came a Nazi dressed in a splendid uniform; he proceeded to segregate us. For some unexplicable reason, I whispered to Zosia not to follow me if we were split up. Of course, being young and small, the so-called doctor took one look at me and pointed to the left. I saw Zosia on the right. Luck was with me. The doctor was distracted by another Nazi. I ran to the right instead. Zosia was overjoyed. She could not believe it. We hugged and shed tears at the same time.

I kept looking toward the men, hoping that Dad and Zenek were together. I saw Zenek, but not Dad. Instead, I noticed a white-haired man standing next to my brother. I was heartbroken. I worried about Zenek being all alone. Not till after the war did I find out that father turned white in an instant.

When the doctors were finished segregating us, soldiers took over. They marched us down a road, which was between huge electric fences. We saw people behind those wires. We were unable to distinguish if they were men or women. Those people were begging us to throw them the bread we carried. To me they looked like inmates in an insane asylum and that is what I told Zosia.

At the end of the road, we were ushered into a red brick building. Waiting for us were males in prison uniforms. The men told us to undress; we were to take a shower. They said that we should put the clothes in a neat pile and jewelry, glasses, and watches on a pile next to the clothes. This way we would be able to find our belongings.

At first, we were too shy to undress in front of the men, but we got scared when they began to threaten us with violence. We did as we were told. Once we were naked, they took us over to a place where we were to be shaved. The men worked in silence, but some of them whispered names of family members they left behind in the Lodz Ghetto, asking if we knew them and if they were with us on the train. One of them seemed to be the boss. He approached me and asked my name. Upon hearing it, he said that he knew my parents. Then he ordered the girl barber not to shave my head, instead just to cut it short. I had long braids, and the scissors were dull. She whispered something about a gas chamber. Just then Zosia appeared, and I told her that she was my sister. The two of us were the only ones left with hair on our heads.

Afterwards, we were led into a huge shower room. We stood and waited for the water to come. Some of the girls must have been told about the gas. While we waited, the women began to scream from fear. It became contagious. I too was screaming, not even knowing why. After a few more seconds, the water came on: we were saved. We left the shower wet and naked. Unabashed, we walked to where the males told us to. There we were each given one garment per person, no underwear, no socks. We did get wooden shoes. I received a long maroon dress. Poor Zosia got a fancy nightgown with a big hole on one breast. None of us received our own clothes. Looking at each other, we realized that now we looked exactly like those inmates we saw on the way in, the ones we thought insane. Zosia and I looked a little better than the rest of the girls, who had their heads shaved.

14

We were then taken to the barracks. Waiting for us at block twenty-six were the "hierarchy" of the home we were to occupy, the queen bee and her aides. She was a Jewish girl from Lodz, but the others were from Hungary. They preceded us by a few months; now they were in charge of Birkenau. A more sinister group of women I have never again come across, with exception of the German women.

Since it was late in the day, they immediately proceeded to assign us to bunk beds, eight or ten to one. It seems to me now to be impossible, but at that time, it was not. We had to lie head to toe. The bunk Zosia and I occupied happened to be on the very top level. Because hot air rises, I began to wheeze again for lack of air. I was convinced that I would suffocate.

The barrack consisted of rows of bunks on each side of the room, in the middle of which was a long narrow concrete stove. We were told to stay on the "beds" or receive a beating. Nevertheless, I climbed down and sat down on the stove. I could stand the beating but not the choking. Within seconds, a horde of "Stubendienst," as the Hungarian workers were called, converged, shouting and ready to kill me for disobeying their orders.

What I'm about to convey may sound impossible or crazy, yet I'm ready to swear that it is the truth. Besides, I have a witness in Zosia as to what happened next. Suddenly, as if in a dream, a little girl appeared, a mere child about five or six; a pretty girl, dressed beautifully, and she had an unexplainable power over the women. She held them at bay, and in perfect Polish told me to stay put. She asked if I was hungry. I was speechless: I nodded. Then she ordered them to bring me food, a pillow, and a blanket. While we waited, she inquired where I was from. She seemed extremely wise and grown up. As soon as I got the things she asked for, she made sure that I would be left alone; then she was gone. I never saw that Angel again. I spent a restful night on my comfortable "bed."

In the morning (about four o'clock) we were awakened by shouts, "Get up for assembly." Once outside, we were told to stay five in a row, alphabetically. Next to us was a woman with two teenage daughters, a Mrs. Randowa. She was not Jewish; her husband, a university professor, was. He was arrested and scheduled for deportation. She and the girls decided to join him, and so they were brought to Lodz Ghetto and consequently to Auschwitz-Birkenau.

We stood in bitter cold for hours waiting to be counted. We huddled together for warmth. When finally the sun came out, the heat was unbearable. Even the climate seemed to be punishing us. When the counting was completed, we were given a piece of bread and black water, which they called coffee. Before we had a chance to eat that "breakfast," we were ordered to the latrine, and if one was lucky to get a seat, with food in tow, we relieved ourselves. At times, before one had a chance to do what comes naturally, we were rushed back to the barracks, where for a while, we were allowed to stay on the floor. I wondered if I would be able to sleep on the stove again.

Over the loud speaker came an announcement asking all children under eighteen to report to the authorities so we could get milk, butter, and possibly eggs. After all the lies the Nazis told, we were still naïve enough to hope that maybe this time they were telling the truth. With Zosia's approval, I and about ten others, including some older ones who, because of malnutrition, could easily have passed for younger, reported. We were taken to what was called a children's barracks. As soon as we entered that place, I had a nagging suspicion. I saw no sleeping bunks, and I regretted that move. There were approximately two hundred of us; we all succumbed to the allure of more and better food. Just as I realized that we were fooled again, a young Hungarian girl came over. She handed me a bucket full of human excrement and ordered me to follow her. She led me to an exit door. She told the German watchman that we were the cleaning crew. He must have known her, so he did not stop us from leaving. As soon as we were out of his sight, she told me to drop the bucket and run after her. She took me back to the barracks; then she stopped and told me to look back. I saw a huge chimney from which flames and smoke were gushing. She said that this was the crematorium. She also told me that all those children they gathered were scheduled to be exterminated next.

When I entered the barracks, I went straight to the bunk where Zosia was anxiously waiting for my return. Dear Zosia; she knew nothing of the children's barrack. Like everyone else, she believed that it was a good thing for us. I had to tell her the truth. She cried and swore that never again were we to part, regardless of any reason, unless we were separated by force. That night I slept on the bunk next to her. We were both scared, and we spent a restless night.

About two AM, Zosia woke me, sobbing. From all that I had told her, she had gotten diarrhea, and there was no way she could hold it much longer. We were in serious trouble. We were closed in, and there was no bathroom or buckets inside. Then I had an idea. Suppose she did in her wooden shoe? There was no other solution and Zosia promptly did so.

When the time came to go out for the counting, we completely forgot that she did it in her shoe. We jumped down from the bunk. Zosia put her feet into the shoes and almost fell; the shoe was so slimy. We laughed about it, and darling Zosia stood with her feet in the dirty shoe. As soon as the counting was finished, instead of going to the latrine, we remained outside and cleaned the shoe with dirt we dug up with our hands and nails.

Then I was surprised by a visit from the same girl that saved me. She brought me a container of warm soup, which I shared with Zosia. She promised to come again. From then on, she appeared every morning, bringing food. One day, while Zosia and I ate greedily, I saw the way Mrs. Randowa and her girls watched as we consumed the food. I knew that they were very hungry, so I decided to share with them from then on.

15

One morning, Mrs. Randowa's older daughter became ill with dysentery. Not having panties, she made right where we stood. Luckily, Ilonka, my Hungarian friend, brought me a pair of warm panties, which I promptly gave to the girl. Once she put them on, she didn't leak fecal matter on the ground; thus, no one beside us knew that she was sick, which saved her from a sure death sentence.

Later on, Ilonka came to see me in the barrack. She took me to the front, where she had a bunk all to herself. I was amazed with the luxury I saw there—silk comforters, silk pillowcases, and lots of food hanging all around. She suggested that I should have her bunk. She told me that she seldom slept there. Her job took her from Birkenau to Auschwitz, where she stayed overnight often. I accepted her offer, providing that Zosia could share with me, which was all right with her. I was curious to know how and why she was able to have all that luxury and was able to walk freely around the camp and why she chose to save me and no other. She explained that I looked exactly like her little sister, who perished in the ovens.

Ilonka then told me that there might be a time when she would not be able to come. If that were to happen, I should go to a little shack not far from the latrine and ask for a man named Ivan, her boyfriend. He knew all about me and would help me. While Zosia and I occupied our luxurious new bunk, I began to feel guilty. Here we were, just the two of us, in all that splendor, while the rest of the women were squeezed like sardines. I told Zosia, and she agreed that we should share our good luck with someone else. We decided on a woman we both knew, whose name was Trudy. She was a friend of Irene's. Upon arriving in Birkenau, she lost her only child, a sweet little girl. She was told by a male inmate to hand over the child to her mother. She did so without realizing why. Though she actually survived, it was at a terrible cost.

When Trudy became aware that she had been tricked to give up her child, she cried constantly. We hoped that we could help her a little by sharing the bunk. Auschwitz-Birkenau was Hell on earth. We lived in constant fear of the next selection for the ovens. If a day passed without selection, it was a miracle.

The selection was conducted by a doctor, Dr Mengele, who was a tall and exceptionally handsome man, often accompanied by a female, a beautiful angel of death. The "good" doctor made them often, in order to make room for the next "shipment"—the new arrivals. At such a time, the girls would pinch my cheeks to give me a little color and give a more healthy look. Somehow, I passed many such encounters. Once he looked closely at me, picked up my chin with his ridding crop and exclaimed, "You will be able to work."

Time after time, my life was spared, while girls in their twenties were put to death. Mrs. Randowa's older daughter was one of them. He took one look at her and told Mrs. Randowa that she would be taken to the infirmary. What fools we mortals are. The mother truly believed the "good" doctor. We had no heart to tell her otherwise.

Ilonka came once again. This time she told me that it would be the last time. She proceeded to explain why. I didn't want to hear it, but she felt that I must know the truth. She worked at the crematorium. The Nazis had a policy that every few months they rotated the workers by getting rid of them in the usual way. Now that her turn was near, she wanted to make sure that I would be taken care of. She made me promise that I would seek out her friend Ivan. After that, I never saw her again. I felt a great sorrow, as though I had lost a loving sister.

A couple of days later, one of the Hungarian girls approached me. She told me that Ivan was asking for me and could not understand why I didn't come to see him. This made me aware that he knew about Ilonka's fate. Why else would he expect me?

That same morning, after the roll call, instead of going to the latrine, I rushed over to the little shack. It was near the Gypsy camp, which was adjacent to ours, separated by an electric fence. I knocked on the door. Someone asked, "What do you want?" I said that I was looking for Ivan. A huge man appeared. He said that he was expecting my visit. He handed me a container of sour pickle soup (I can still smell it), a chunk of bread, and a whole Polish kielbasa. I thanked him and asked him if he knew what happened to Ilonka. He looked at me sadly and nodded his head. Then he spoke up, "We don't ask such questions here." And he asked me to come again whenever I could.

On my way back, a loud speaker announced a "Blockspare." All inmates were to stay locked up in their barracks. Within seconds, I found myself alone. There was Pieroshka (the redhead) running toward me, a devil personified. We pitied anyone that she caught doing something that was prohibited. I was forced to do something drastic, or I would be her next victim. I dashed into the nearest barracks. As I entered, a big Hungarian woman grabbed my arm, screaming, "You don't belong here." I offered her my goodies. She took the bread and kielbasa but left me the soup. Then she hid me behind her bunk bed. I stood there literally shaking in my wooden clogs. Pieroshka entered and looked around. Luckily she didn't see me. As soon as the lock-in was over, I ran to block twenty-six, where Zosia was beside herself waiting for me. I told her about Ivan and about my almost deadly encounter with the redhead. Then Zosia swore that she would never allow me to go anywhere again. We enjoyed the soup while I was still shaking as I slurped it.

16

There was a time when standing for the roll call, we waited and waited, not knowing the reason for the delay. We were hungry and very thirsty. We begged the "Kapo" for some water, but she refused. She told us that it was prohibited for her to give us anything. That woman proved to be a mean bitch. She took delight in telling us that we would be gassed and that we were not given a tattooed number because we were not fit for work. We heard it before from other inmates.

As we stood waiting, a couple of Polish men who worked at the women's camp passed by. Some girls asked them to bring us water. The men left and soon came back with two pitchers of clear water. They gave them to the girls. Soon the rest of them began to fight for it. The Kapo, seeing the reason for the disturbance, shouted for help, and no other than Pieroshka herself came. She pulled the pitchers out of the hands of the women and spilt that precious liquid. Then she surprised us by sitting down on the ground and beginning to cry. Through tears, she began to talk, telling us that when she arrived from Hungary with her family, they were all taken to the gas chambers, where she watched as her father, mother, and siblings were dying. For an unexplainable reason, she did not affected by the gassing. When the Germans found that she was alive, they were so amazed that they decided to let her live. They rewarded her by making her a head Kapo. Now she was devoid of any feelings, and she served them well.

Finally the Nazis came. They finished the counting and we were free to go to the latrine. As we passed the Gypsy camp, we were surprised to see that it was empty. During the night the Nazis had taken them all to the crematorium.

The Nazis were now anxious to get rid of us, as many as they possibly could. The selections intensified. The ovens were working overtime, day and night. Forty thousand a day perished. The whole of Birkenau reeked of burning flesh. There was no longer any doubt in our minds. We now knew all that previously we could not believe and did not want to accept. We dragged along, trying not to think about the horrors we witnessed. It's impossible to convey the fear we felt when, after a roll call, we were told to remain standing. That happened only when an inmate went missing. Sometimes a desperate girl would throw herself on the electric wire, and it would take time to discover the charred body.

We knew that something was amiss, especially since the other barracks were discharged. We feared that, as the Hungarian women always warned us, we would be the next ones to go. Waiting in unbearable heat for hours for whatever, finally we were told that we were being taken on a trip. By then we were ready for anything; we were just too tired physically and mentally, and we were prepared to accept what would happen.

We were rounded up. Silently we marched, surrounded by guards and snarling dogs. Then we were left standing, while the guards had lunch in a nearby hut. Out of nowhere, a woman appeared. She addressed us in Czech, asking if there were Slovaks among us. Mrs. Randowa told her that she was from Prague. The two of them conversed for a while. After the woman left, Mrs. Randowa eased our fears by telling us what she was told. It seemed that, indeed, we were standing at a railroad station, which meant that we were really and truly leaving this hell on earth alive. The woman came back, bringing bread and a salami for Mrs. Randowa, which she promptly shared with Zosia and me. In truth, we didn't give much credence to this; we had been told enough lies to last us a lifetime.

Some time later, we heard a train whistle, and we saw a cattle train approaching. Sure enough, it stopped. The guards returned and began to hand dresses out to us. Once this was done, they rushed us into the train. Again, the cars were filled to capacity. We didn't care; we were happy to leave this Gehenna.

The ride seemed endless. We stopped somewhere where we received soup, but once again no water or any other liquids. The cars were freezing. We became dehydrated, so much so that when we finally arrived to our destination, the soldiers that took over from the guards assumed that we were drunk. We were unable to stand or walk a straight line.

We marched through small villages and farms. We came across a hog farm. There were wooden rails filled with dirty water, probably for the pigs. We attacked that water with vehemence. The "nice" farmers began to pelt us with stones and yelled, "You filthy Jews." Lucky that they didn't have guns, otherwise they would have shot us. It amazed me how much hatred they displayed.

It took about two hours, walking through a dense forest. We saw no fences. We arrived at a place called Bergen-Belzen. Here we were taken into a brick building reminiscent of the one in Birkenau and we were told to undress. We became uneasy, especially when they told us that we were going to shower and go through a process called delousing. The only difference was this time we had no luggage or jewelry. Mrs. Randowa calmed us by rationalizing that they would not take us all this way in order to kill us, when they could do it in Birkenau.

After we showered, we put on the same rags we came in. Again, we marched about a mile. We arrived at a clearing still in the forest. We were told that this was the place where we would spend the night. No blankets. Nothing but tall grass and dew. After a sleepless night, we welcomed the morning. We looked about. To our surprise, we realized that we were not fenced in, and the clearing was full of stale bread. Hungrily, we attacked it with zest.

The guards came and led us to the camp, where there were no barracks, only a couple of tents, which were to house us. Inside on the bare ground was some straw. We each claimed our territory. Zosia and I would lie next to Mrs. Randowa and her now only daughter. We were given aluminum cans, which we could use as dishes. Next we were ushered outside and given food, bread with jam. If there was such a thing as Paradise, then this was it.

17

The first roll call in Bergen-Belzen. Because of my size and age, the women made me stay in the back, the tall girls in front of me trying to hide me. The counting was conducted by a female guard. We took it as a bad omen, since our experience in Auschwitz taught us that women were more vicious than men. The one that counted us looked exceptionally mean. We were filled with trepidation, expecting the worst. As she approached the end of the line, she stopped and glared at me, then continued. I was frightened, and the girls were sure that this would be the end for me. I felt like Marie Antoinette standing at the Guillotine.

At noontime she appeared in the tent. She walked slowly, deliberately, as if looking for someone. Instinctively I knew that she was searching for me. She spotted me and indicated that I should follow her outside. There was nothing I could do. I had to do her bidding. Terrified I followed her. She stopped, looked at me and spoke for the first time. "Little one, do you know how to pluck eyebrows or squeeze out blackheads?" I thought quickly. "I did it for my sister," I replied in perfect German. "I used to do it for my sister Irene." Of course I lied, but I used to watch Zosia performing the task.

As if it were an omen, she repeated my sister's name. "Irene," she said. "This is also my name. Irene Hesce." She said this in Polish. She told me that she was born and raised in Silesia, a Polish province, but she did not speak it as well as German. After this exchange, she said that starting tomorrow, I shall work for her. Then she told me to go back to the tent. Elated, I think that I flew back to where the girls were fearfully waiting for my return. I related what had transpired. They were relieved and very happy for me. Those women regarded at me as the child or siblings they had lost. To them I represented them all.

That evening, as I approached the girl whose job was dishing out soup, the wardress Irene took the ladle, dug deep into the kettle, and gave me the thickest soup I had ever gotten. That night we all went to sleep satisfied; I with a full belly, and the rest of them tranquil, now that their fears for my life were put to rest, for a while, anyhow.

In the morning, the Nazis asked us to choose a Lagerfuhrer (one In charge). We decided on Mrs. Randowa as a Lagerfuhrer and a Mrs. Lernerowa for the 'blokowa.' Both ladies spoke German fluently. Besides, they seemed to be the oldest, about forty.

After the roll call, the wardress Irene came for me. She brought a blanket and tweezers. We went to the clearing. Once there, she lay down, and I very carefully plucked her brows. Next, I squeezed her blackheads—she had a lot. She was satisfied and rewarded me with a slab of bread and a thick piece of pork. I ate only a small piece. The rest I saved for Zosia. She was impressed with my selflessness. It became a daily routine. I did it for about one hour a day, and she always had something for me. I was the only one "working," while the rest spent the days wandering aimlessly.

Soon the weather changed. It turned cold and windy, so much so that we could not continue. The winds tore the tents and did damage to "our home." Irene inquired if I knew how to sew. I told her about my work at the factory. She was pleased. She gave me a new job. I was to be in charge of a sewing circle, mending the torn tent material. She chose nine more girls. It was not an easy task. The cloth was coarse and extremely hard to sew. We worked with special needles and heavy thread. Irene gave me scissors and made it clear that no one besides me was to handle them. Somehow we did it and even became proficient. Day after day, in bitter cold, we sat mending the cloth. The weather was getting worse by the day. We had plenty of work. The place where we sat became muddy; then it froze. It was hard to sew. Our fingers were ice cold; we could barely hold the needles.

18

One day while we worked, a group of Nazis came to check on our progress. Unbeknownst to us, one of them was the infamous Dr. Kramer. The "good" Dr. stared at the girl sitting next to me. He asked if we were sisters. Everyone looked scared, unable to speak, but I, with my big mouth, looked him straight in the eyes and answered. "No. Not that we are aware of, unless my dad strayed." All the Nazis burst out laughing. Again he spoke, this time only to me. "Little Devil, are you hungry?" he asked. Bravely I replied, "Yes, mein Herr." "Tell me then, how many soups could you consume?" Foolishly, I said five. I could eat five. "Well then, you shall have five, but you must eat them all. We do not waste food," he proclaimed.

He waited till noontime and ordered the 'widzielaczka' to dish out five portions for me. Greedily, I started the feast only to stop at the third one, my eyes being bigger than my stomach. I could not swallow another drop. I tried, but to no avail. Watching me struggle, he said, "Don't ever overestimate your capabilities." And he walked away. I expected to be punished severely. For the first few moments I did not realize what happened. I was trembling with fear and could not stop. Then I composed myself and began to laugh hysterically. Two hundred women watched it; even the guards heard about it. The wardress Irene thought that I took too much liberty with such an important man as Herr Doctor. Nevertheless, I felt that she was impressed with my boldness.

That same day, she gave me a new present. It was a big powder case with a mirror and a real comb. I was now the richest girl in the camp and the envy of all. Every morning, the powder case made the rounds. We hadn't seen ourselves since we left the Ghetto. The first time it was a shock, especially for the women whose heads were shaven, even though they were sprouting some of it back. I was selfish and glad that they didn't have more hair. So, the comb was used by Zosia and me.

The day after the incident with the soup, we were told to wrap up the cloth and supplies—our work was finished. The women asked to keep some of the scraps; they would use them for bras or panties. I was against it, and I told them so, but they would not listen. Even Zosia wanted a few pieces. When I refused, she became upset with me. Somehow I had a gut feeling about it. I was right. The Germans became aware of it. They came into the tent and conducted a search for the contraband. They became enraged when they found it. All those who possessed some scraps were arrested, including Mrs. Randowa. She received a little bag made of the precious cloth. I was not aware that some girls had been hoarding it all along. I considered myself lucky that I didn't have anything made of the tent material and that I was mean to Zosia.

Overnight, the Germans had Russian prisoners build a special camp. All the guilty women were confined there. The thieves had to haul stones around and around, twenty-four hours, night and day. We, the innocent, were also punished—no food or water for three days. The Nazis were fond of saying, "All for one and one for all." For the next two days, Zosia and I took turns licking a small piece of margarine that we saved from the food the wardress Irene gave me.

The third day, the hunger and thirst became unbearable. We were locked in. Regardless, I decided to venture out to try and do some "organizing," which in the camp lingo meant stealing. I asked Edzia, one of the girls who shared the sleeping quarters with us, to go with me. Because we each had one blanket, we figured that by sleeping together, we could use a couple on the cold ground and use the other one to cover ourselves with. Sleeping together, we also had the heat of our bodies to keep us warm.

As we went outside the tent, we were astonished by the changes that had taken place in only a couple of days. There were many more tents on the grounds. Those were occupied by new arrivals, mostly Hungarians, with a few Polish girls. They must have had the Russian prisoners put more tents them up. Trains must have brought them at night. We visited tent after tent, hoping to find relatives or friends. There was always a chance that someone might have survived. The only one I came across was the principal of the school I had attended. Her name was Dr. Serr. Once a very pretty lady, now she looked old and decrepit. She was skeletal. I found it depressing, especially when she begged me for food.

I ran out of that tent, tears rolling down my cheeks and a lump in my throat. We continued looking but now only for a scrap of food. Just when the new arrivals were being fed the proverbial soup. We stood in line, hoping that no one would take notice and realize that we didn't belong. No such luck. We were told to get lost, otherwise they would report us to the guards.

Despondent, we started the trek back. On the way, we spotted a couple of new arrivals dragging a kettle of soup. It was obvious to us that they were lost. Edzia asked if there was anything wrong. The poor girls admitted that they could not find the tent that they were supposed to bring the soup to. Edzia suggested that they go and find the tent while we watched the kettle. The naïve girls even thanked us and went in search of their new home. As soon as they left, Edzia looked at me. I knew what she had in mind. If truth must be told, I felt a little guilty. Only a little, but hunger is more powerful than conscience. We grabbed the kettle and away we went. We entered our tent with as much aplomb as Cleopatra entering Rome. The girls admired our nerve. Zosia was as hungry as she was worried about my taking so many chances. She told me that I was either stupid or brave, most likely stupid, and that she would rather starve than lose me. Nevertheless, all participated in the feast and all went to sleep satisfied. No more hunger pains.

19

One day, while watching the Russian inmates working, I was curious to find out where they were getting the supplies. There was always a chance of organizing something valuable. As I tailed them, I discovered a camp not far from ours. I never before knew that there was a different Lager beside ours, as unbelievable as the one I now discovered. There were men and women together, even children. I thought that I was dreaming. I parked myself at the fence and tried to speak with them. They spoke a little German, and I was able to find out that they were Jews from Holland. They said that they were waiting to be exchanged and emigrate to America. I could not believe it; yet watching them, I realized that they didn't look anything like us. Those people were dressed in normal clothes, hats, and shoes. The men had beards, and the women were not shorn as we were.

I hurried back and related it all to my friends. They listened in amazement, not ready to accept it. I decided to take them there and let them see for themselves, but it would be impossible to do it that day. The next morning, I took them there. Unfortunately when we got there, the camp was empty, only barracks remained. The girls were sure that I dreamed the whole thing up. If it weren't for the Russian prisoners who attested to it, the girls would have been sure that I was hallucinating. We wondered what happened to them, hoping that indeed they were on their way to the States.

20

Our tents were not built to withstand the freezing and the winds; thus, we were moved to new quarters. This time we were housed in straw huts. They were a little more livable; still we slept on the ground. The only luxury we had was running water, which was located outside. I was not sure if the wardress Irene would be there.

Not being one to accept what was being dished out, I schemed up a plan to impress the new wardress. On the first morning, I got up way before any one else. It was still dark, and the whole camp was asleep. I undressed and, with the ice-cold water, washed my body, even my hair. Then I combed my tresses, cleaned the blanket from the straw, and folded it neatly. All the while, I was aware that the wardress on duty was watching, fascinated. The Fraulein was impressed, and I got myself a new protector. Mission accomplished. Again I was singled out and given a job. This time I was made a translator and a gatekeeper. I was the first to be fed and always received a little more than the rest. I was also allowed to roam the grounds.

One day, I met a girl I knew in the Ghetto. She told me that her mom was with her until she became ill. The Germans took her to the infirmary. Cathy asked me to go and see her, but not before the meal. She gave me the soup that she saved for her mother. I was touched by her willingness to sacrifice. As hungry as she probably was, she wanted her mother to have it. I gladly took the soup and went to deliver the precious gift. I entered the infirmary and looked for her mom. I could not find her. I asked one of the nurses. She told me that the lady had expired that same morning. I gave the soup to someone else, and I never told Cathy.

One day we were surprised; we were to get new clothes. Most likely those that were taken from new arrivals. We stood in line, and as we approached, a new wardress handed us whatever she grabbed. Afraid that I might get a flimsy one, I took matters in my own hands, but only after I received a thin silk dress. Instead of leaving with it, I crawled in the tall grass under the table where the dresses lay. I proceeded to feel the sleeves that were hanging down, seeking a woolen one. Upon finding it, I began to pull on the dress, only to drag the rest of them with it. Amazed, the wardress looked down and found me clutching the woolen dress. She didn't think that it was funny. She pulled me out and proceeded to slap my face. She wore leather gloves, which stung and left red welts. Nevertheless, it was worth it, for I was allowed to keep the warm dress.

There was always a reason the Nazis did something "nice" like giving us better clothes. Soon after, we found out. "Buyers" came looking for new slave workers. Every day we stood for inspection, and they chose the girls. I was in charge of the list, and, in my capacity as a translator, I would call out the names of the victims.

Meanwhile, Zosia met a girlfriend who was chosen for work. Zosia suddenly decided that she, too, wanted to go. She also tried to convince me to join them. I would not do such a thing unless I spoke to the wardress. After I asked, I was told to stay put. She told me, "You will get little to eat and lots of beatings." I asked her what to do about my sister who by then had volunteered. The wardress suggested that I don't call Zosia's name; she would help by taking someone else instead. I had no choice; I did what I was told. At first Zosia was mad at me, but shortly after, the workers were shipped back, sick with tuberculosis. They worked in ammunition factories. Being underground with lack of air and the poor food did them in. Zosia's friend was one of them.

21

Nothing ever stays the same for long. As soon as we felt "at home," we got moved again. Now they moved us into regular wooden barracks. We entered the old grounds and were astonished at the vastness of it. Hundreds of barracks and thousands of prisoners; it was just like being in Auschwitz, that hellish place.

We were assigned to a bunk located at the very top. We shared it with eight others: Mrs. Randowa; her daughter, Helga; Zosia's best friend, Bella; her sister, Dincia; two of their cousins, Itka and Adela; plus their sister-in-law, a woman of about thirty-five. We called her mama. And, of course, Zosia and I. There was a light bulb over our bunk; the only one in the whole place.

On the first night, we were attacked by unbelievably huge rats. All that night, we heard moans groans and screams. The place was overrun by those beasts. We were afraid to go to sleep. We devised a way to keep them away: we slept in shifts and rattled our cans to hold them at bay. After many sleepless nights, we walked like Zombies. Our food rations were shrinking with each new arrival. I was worried as never before, convinced that this was the end for all of us.

By day, I roamed the grounds, looking for something to organize, but no such luck. Then I came across a couple of women munching on a piece of meat. I began to follow them, thinking that they were stealing it from the kitchen. If so, then I could do likewise. I walked a few feet behind them. They probably noticed me, but they didn't seem to mind, which struck me as odd. Suddenly, I saw a pile of cadavers, and the women were heading right for it. Instinctively, I backed away. I realized where the meat was coming from. I ran back, sobbing all the way. I felt ashamed for them and the sorry state we were reduced to.

Every time I thought that we had gotten to our ultimate degradation, more horrible things would occur. Despondent, I headed straight for the bunk where Zosia and the rest of the women sat listless. The combination of sleeplessness and hunger was just too much. We didn't even have strength to converse, which was okay by me. I didn't want to talk and did not intend to tell them anything of what I witnessed. That night I stayed awake afraid that I might see the dismembered corpses in my dreams.

At dawn, I ventured out again. I just could not stay around the girls for fear of what I might divulge to them. I wandered aimlessly. I came across a classmate. I hardly recognized her and would surely have passed her by, except that she called me by name. I was shocked to see her. In the ghetto, she was already sick with TB. How she made it so far was a mystery, yet I knew that she would not survive long and neither would I. We exchanged a few words. I left her sitting on the cold ground shivering.

That night, Helga, Mrs. Randowa's daughter, woke me up crying and begged me to accompany her to the latrine. That place was a long way off. It was nothing but a hole in the ground surrounded by wooden logs, which we used for support and to protect us from falling in. We all knew that many newborn babies were disposed of that way by their mothers. Women who were pregnant preferred to do that rather then have the Nazis murder their innocent babes. It was still dark as we started to walk. The only light that was there was from the guards' huts. We hiked close to the fence. Suddenly, a German began to shoot at us. Most likely he thought that we were trying to escape. One of the bullets grazed my right calf. Helga was not hurt physically, only mentally. She got so scared that she soiled herself.

Mrs. Randowa checked my wound. She suggested that I cleanse it with my own urine to prevent infection. For that task, I had to use my aluminum can. My wound never got infected. Now I was marred in two places, one on my leg, the other one on my face (from the beating). Since we moved, I had not seen my "friend," Irene. Without her, I was just another inmate.

When my mom was taken away from us, I thought that I was all cried out. But now, after the occurrences with the two women and meeting my ex-classmate, I wept all the time. It helped a little to be able to cry again, and I realized that I was still a human being, but I cried only when I was away from the girls. I entered the barracks and found the place in an uproar. Zosia was so excited that she didn't even noticed my swollen red eyes. She hurried over to tell me that, while I was gone, the buyers came and ordered all to get ready for deportation. This time there was to be no selection—all two hundred girls, they were taking all of us.

The wardress Irene came. She took me aside and told me not to worry. We were going deep into Germany to a place called Saxenhausen to work in a curtain factory. I really did not believe it, but I accepted that tale. We said our goodbyes and I thanked her for all that she did for me. Then I told the girls how lucky we were. According to Irene, it was a very nice country town where the plant was located, and the work was easy.

We were taken to a different barracks, where we were given coats. This was such an unexpected act, nothing like that had happened before, and we felt sure that nothing bad would befall us. They would not bother to dress us if they intended to kill us. The coat I got was a very pretty one—it was gray with a fur collar, and it would have been a real prize if it was not for the red stripe that was painted on the back with the letters K.L standing for Konzentrationslager.

22

Once more we were taken to a railroad station by guards with the proverbial German shepherds. While we waited to be shipped out, we received some soup brought by Russian inmates.

One of the girls asked for my compact. She wanted to look at herself. Knowing what would ensue, I refused. She became belligerent, calling me all kinds of names. Zosia became upset and ordered me to let her have that priceless little glass. I handed her the compact and, as I expected, it began to make the rounds. A guard, a particularly vicious one, spotted it and demanded to know where the girls had stolen it from. The one holding it got scared, and she was unable to utter a word. The guard began to beat her mercilessly, all the while shouting for her to confess to the crime.

I could not take it any longer. Afraid for the girl's life, I stepped forward and admitted to being the owner. He grabbed me by my hair, which by now was long. "Who did you steal it from?" he yelled, his face was red as a beet. Once more, my luck held out. The wardress Irene was nearby and hearing the commotion, she stepped in and admitted giving it to me, whereupon he stormed out, cursing under his breath. At that point, the other guards came in and told us that the trains were ready and waiting. Irene waved goodbye, wished me luck, and walked away. I wondered how one can be so nice to me and so cruel to others.

We boarded a cattle train once more, except that this time we had a guard in each wagon, who kept the doors open. I suppose he could not stand the smell of so many women that hadn't washed for days. It was freezing, but at least we had fresh air. The guard was very talkative. We thought that he was a little bit retarded, especially when he admitted to being present at the time when we arrived at Bergen-Belzen. He could not understand how we could drink the dirty water, and what's more, how we undressed with so many guards watching. He also added that he had been married for twenty-five years and had never seen his wife naked. I suppose he had never been either thirsty or filthy.

The train made some stops, mainly to take on water. It then that we cleaned the car and emptied the buckets of excrement. At times, we were stranded in the middle of nowhere. Some of the rails were destroyed by bombs. That is when we realized that the allied forces were fighting in earnest, and that we were not alone. At those times, we had to wait while Russian prisoners did the repairs. Again, I wondered whose sons and husbands they were, those tired and undernourished men.

At other times, we rode through lovely little villages. Once, as the train came really close to some houses, I saw people looking out from windows adorned with lacy curtains. I ached to be able, once more in my life, to look through a window with curtains. More than anything else, it made me think of home and family. To dwell on those memories was painful and dangerous. If one were to survive, one had to think only of the here and now. That is how I became obsessed with windows.

Meanwhile, we spent our time wondering what was waiting for us this time. I do not know how long the trip lasted, since time was irrelevant for us. Finally, we arrived at a small station, and we were told to disembark. This done, we were marched in very deep snow perhaps for a mile or two. We came to a stop in front of a big building. We noticed that there were no fences or guards, only the men that brought us. We were taken inside. We walked up a flight of stairs and entered a big room. There were bunks along the walls, and we were told that this is the place we would live and work in.

We were shown a big washroom with sinks with running hot and cold water. Next, we were introduced to the toilet. It consisted of thirteen holes and wooden seats. Then we heard a hissing noise, and discovered that the room had central heating. Such a luxury we did not expect after the death camps. Exhausted, we chose our beds and went to sleep.

We lay down on the bunks and before we had a chance to rest, a couple of Frauleins, accompanied by guards, came in carrying a kettle of hot soup. Since we never parted with our "dishes," we were given the nourishment, which we drank greedily (we had no spoons). We were also given nice blankets and told to go to sleep. We fell asleep, only to wake up with horrendous pains in the legs. All of us were afflicted with it. We didn't understand what was happening. The pain was excruciating. At daylight, we discovered that our toes had turned black as coal. We were not able to stand, much less walk.

The commandant was summoned. He came to see what was wrong with us. After seeing our toes, he became angry, not so much with us as with the buyers for delivering him damaged goods.

One of the Frauleins suggested summoning a doctor. Soon one came, accompanied by a nurse in a white uniform. He examined some of the girls and declared that we would be useless. Our feet were frostbitten, and he knew of no medicine that could help. He advised the commandant to get rid of us pronto. The same German girl who called the doctor was astounded. She asked the doctor if he was a National Socialist or a Nazi. If a Nazi, then he was no doctor. He didn't answer but left in a huff.

We listened to this exchange in amazement. Were there really people in Germany that had the guts to stand up to the Nazis? If so, then maybe there was a chance for humanity to wake up. But when? Would it happen while we were still alive? Those thoughts were making me dizzy with hope.

Then the same Fraulein spoke to the Kommandant, telling him that she knew a famous country healer who lived in her village, not far from the factory. She would be happy to fetch him. The distraught Kommandant agreed. He had no other choice but to protect his investment. He must have paid a lot of marks for us.

At noontime, she came back, and the healer was with her. He brought with him a huge earthen pot filled with a salve. He distributed it to us. He also gave us strips of torn blankets, with instructions to bandage the legs after applying the salve. That was the most painful night ever. The combination of the salve and the heat from the woolen strips was unbearable. I remember pulling my hair out from the severe pain. I was not alone. Zosia and the rest of the girls were going through the same tortures. The pain lasted three days; then it slowly subsided. The flesh began to heal. Within a week the blood began to circulate and the toes regained some color. The commandant was elated, but not us much as we. We were happy to be alive and not feeling pain.

While we were recuperating, we wondered about the work we were slated for. One evening, a wardress came. She asked for a volunteer. She had some work for only one girl. Since no one did, I felt obliged to do so, in order to save face. I didn't want her to think that we were a lazy bunch.

She took me downstairs, where she had a room. The radiator was leaking, and she needed me to wipe up the mess. She even helped with the chore. She was friendly and talkative. She asked many questions. One of them was what I did wrong that at such a young age I was incarcerated. She really thought that I had committed some hideous crime. Not realizing that she really didn't know, I told her that I killed my mother. Of course, I said it ironically. I did not know if she believed me. She said that she was sorry, and she rewarded me for a job well done, a big slice of bread spread with real butter and a small dish with jam. As always, I didn't eat it. I took it with me to share with Zosia.

In retrospect, I now believe that some of the Germans didn't know about the death camps, especially the ones that were far removed from them, since most of the camps were located on Polish soil, aided and abetted by Polish, Hungarian, and Slovak collaborators. She escorted me back to our quarters. I had to tell the women what I had to do and what I told her.

By morning, Mrs. Randowa was told by the commandant to pick a few women for work in the kitchen. Mrs. Randowa asked him for permission to allow her to place the youngest girls. She would like them to be employed there. I was one of the five she picked. The chefs were two older women, one who claimed to be a cook (in reality was the madam of a whorehouse) and Vera, the one that shared the bunk in Auschwitz with Zosia and me. The wardress in charge of the kitchen was the one I wiped the floor for. She was pleased to see me and said so.

The kitchen was divided into two parts, one for the inmates and the other for Germans. Our duty was to keep it clean and do all the odd jobs, like peeling potatoes and making sure that the vegetables were washed and chopped, weighing the portions of bread and brewing the ersatz coffee. The Germans were also rationed, except that they were given three times as much as we.

23

Our work required that we start at five each morning, thus we were exempt from roll call. In the meanwhile, the girls waited for the factory to be opened. Still no one knew what kind of work awaited them. The conversation was rampant with rumors. The only thing for sure was that it wouldn't be the dreaded ammunition. One day, when I came back after my work in the kitchen was finished, I found Zosia in tears. It seemed that the Germans asked for volunteers to do an odd job. Since my experience was such a winning one, the girls, including Zosia, were anxious to enlist. Unfortunately, the work consisted of unloading trucks with parts of machinery that were to be installed in the factory. The temperature was below freezing. The steel parts were so cold that they would stick to their bare hands, and once again the women got frostbite. Their flesh was raw, and it was extremely painful. Again, the girls had to apply the miracle salve. Luckily, their hands healed before the plant opened.

The women were taught to operate the heavy machinery under the tutorage of German Meisters. Afterwards, they worked in shifts, one group in daytime and the other at night. Thus the plant was operating full blast, building parts for planes and tanks for our most despised enemy. Yet considering our previous experiences, this place was Eden.

The wardresses (except two) were pretty easy on us. The Kommandant was not too bad, either. He was fond of telling us how lucky we were, having thirteen holes in the lavatory. Thus, we referred to the toilet as "the thirteen holes." Sometimes we were even taken into the yard for exercise or to play ball, but most of the time we had to march in a circle, which we dreaded. The reason being that among us was a girl lucky enough to still have her mother—a miracle. That poor woman had absolutely no coordination. She was unable to catch a ball or march in step with the rest of us.

As luck would have it, the wardress responsible for our exercise was one of the meanest bitches. She would go to work on that poor woman. She delighted in beating her mercilessly, until she passed out. Then she would order her daughter to throw cold water, to revive her, only to be able to punish her again and again, while we stood by unable to help. Strangely enough, the same wardress herself walked with a limp.

All in all, as I remember, that place was not too bad. We became used to the unpleasantness and enjoyed the "good" moments. We considered ourselves extremely lucky.

One of the worst things was that no one could go relieve herself without permission, especially at night. Because our diet was so poor, we constantly had to go to pee. At such a time, one had to wake the wardress on duty, report the reason for having to go, and ask to be allowed to use the thirteen holes. Then it depended on the wardress. If she was amicable, then it was okay, and if not, one could sneak out without her permission. I was never able to do it. My walk was, and still is a heavy one; thus, when I tried it, I would wake her up and receive a tongue lashing and at times had to wait till morning. Believe me, it was hard.

The factory workers used to tell us that even there they had to ask permission, and if it wasn't given, they would hide behind the machines and do it right there. Some of the "Meisters" complained that there was a bad odor coming from the girls, and that they had to wash more often. If only they knew the true reason. Still they cursed the girls for having weak bladders: "Eure verdamte Bladden" (Your damned bladders).

24

The Nazis must have lost a lot of planes and tanks. They were expanding the factory. One hundred and fifty Hungarians were brought in. Among them was one Polish Jewess. Her name was Lola, and she was by far the most beautiful girl there. She hailed from a Town called Katowice. She came via Auschwitz, where she had an important job (whatever it was). The rumor was that she was a mistress of an important Nazi, and it was said that she had in her possession a letter from the said Nazi, giving her special protection. She arrived wearing beautiful clothes, including leather boots which was unheard of in the camps.

Lola was in charge of the Hungarian women. She ruled them, much the same as the wardresses in Auschwitz. Lola tried to convince us that it would be good for us to let her be in charge of the whole camp. We didn't buy it. We were happy with the way Mrs. Randowa ran our part of the camp. It didn't take Lola long to become our Kommandant's mistress. She persuaded him to allow the Hungarian girls to visit us on Sundays (they occupied the third floor). It turned out to be nice for all of us. We entertained them, and they in turn put on shows for us. Even the wardresses enjoyed the performances. For a while, we felt human again.

One of the shows we held was a presentation of what was. We made miniature clothes, even make-believe pastries. The clothes were made by a girl who was a dressmaker, and we baked the cakes in the kitchen from crumbs of bread and stolen sugar from the German provisions. The show was quite a hit.

Other times we sang and danced. The songs were in Jewish and very nostalgic. At times, even the German women asked us to sing some of their tunes which reminded them of their homes and made them cry.

One day, the German women presented us with a terrible dilemma. It seemed that our "good" Kommandant was stealing from their food rations as well as from ours and selling them on the black market. The wardresses told us that they would write to the International Red Cross with those accusations, but they needed us to sign the petition. For us it was a no-win situation. Damned if we do or damned if we don't. Because they were in charge of our well-being day and night, we were forced to oblige. We worried about the Kommandant's reaction. Mrs. Randowa suggested that if and when the delegation comes and questions us, we should be cagey and answer only with one sentence, "We have thirteen holes."

The fateful day arrived. We stood in a circle and were bombarded with many questions. Again and again we repeated, "We have thirteen holes," hoping that the distinguished Swedish bureaucrats would catch on and see how frightened we were. No such luck. They really were not interested in us. They didn't care and found the whole thing amusing. Thus, with a happy and laughing Kommandant, they went off to have lunch at his home. Well, so much for the International Red Cross. Nothing was done for us or the German women.

25

I would be remiss not to admit that among us there were some squabbles. Nothing earth shaking, but at times unpleasant.

The seamstress was very good, and the wardresses wasted no time in taking advantage of her capabilities. They supplied her with a sewing machine, materials, and all the necessary things needed. In the evenings after work, she would sew clothes for them. A girl, who shall remain nameless (for a good reason), had asked the seamstress for some scraps of material. Remembering the fiasco in Bergen-Belzen, she refused, afraid of the consequences. She declined and didn't give her the "shmates." The errant girl became mad at the woman and did something ugly. She stole the little black book where the seamstress kept the necessary measurements of her "customers." Since she didn't know their given names, she used nicknames; some flattering, but most of them not. The enraged girl handed over the little book to one of the mean wardresses, hoping to get the poor girl in trouble. That the dirty act backfired. Most of the Frauleins were flattered by the names the seamstress attributed to them, especially when they were told that the names belonged to famous Polish actresses.

The camp was in an uproar. We liked the seamstress and felt sorry for her. All of us knew that she lost her only baby on arrival in Auschwitz. She suffered for a long time and was terribly depressed. We feared for her a long time. Now that she was sought out and appreciated, she forgot (if one can). We didn't like what the girl did, and she well knew it. She was ostracized by all until she realized what she had done. She apologized to her and to us all.

26

Just when I thought that life, such as it was, was becoming bearable, a new calamity befell me. On one "nice" day, in marched the Kommandant. He headed straight for me shouting. "You lied to the German government," he yelled. "You will be punished severely. Most likely we'll hang you!" he screamed. Then he ran out like one amok. I was left speechless, bewildered. I didn't know what he meant, and did not recall any such thing.

The wardress, Lisette (by now I knew her name), upon hearing the commotion, came in and asked me what all this was about. I told her that I had no idea. She believed me and went out. Unbeknown to me, she took it upon herself to find out. In the meantime, I was still working, while the Germans were hard at work building a gallows.

What masters of deceit the Nazis were. The bad news spread like wildfire. Zosia was inconsolable, while I was stunned. Mrs. Randowa did her best for me. She spoke to the commandant; he was adamant. He still insisted that I committed a crime. I think that I was the only calm person during the whole farce. Either I was stupid or too young to realize the danger I was in. As the saying goes, God looks out for fools. The wardress, Lisette, came to my rescue by checking the files (yes, they kept them). She discovered that at the time, I was in the children's barrack. I gave my true age. Upon Ilonka's advice, I had given my age as eighteen when leaving Auschwitz-Birkenau. Then Mrs. Randowa, in order to have me work in the kitchen, gave the commandant my real age. Their excellent record-keeping revealed all. Learning all that, the wardress Lisette managed to get me out of that terrible predicament. It boggles the mind how the Nazis kept such implacable records while murdering so many. One wonders to what purpose. All I know is that I definitely had a guardian Angel.

27

A day came when we were being bombed. We were delighted. Finally we got what we were praying for. We didn't care for our safety; all we cared about was knowing that someone, somewhere, was doing something for us. During those raids we were locked up, while the Germans hid in bunkers. Nothing much happened, and nothing we heard made us think that the Nazis suffered physically, but we were sure that mentally they did.

In the meantime, we had no water or deliveries from the bakery or any other suppliers, but we were used to being without, while the Nazi's weren't. Their rations had to be only half of what they were getting prior to the bombing. Even their soups were not as rich as before.

And once, while we carried the kettle in order to deliver it to them, one of the girls tripped and we spilled the whole kettle. We were at a loss about what to do. Basia, the main cook, told us to scoop up the mess and refill the kettle with the dirty soup. We did as we were told, and what was left on the floor we ate. That's how precious food was to us.

One day, while I was in the provision room sitting in a potato bin, the wardress Lisette, accompanied by another one, walked into the room. Unaware that I was there, they spoke about air raids and about the sorry way the war was progressing (for them). They spoke about the shortage of food, especially salt, which by now was scarce, and that the Russian army was close to the town of Meltore, the one we "lived" in. I sat quietly, afraid of letting them know that I heard the whole conversation. As soon as they left, I stuffed my pockets with the precious salt, picked up the basket of potatoes and sneaked back into the kitchen. I repeated what I had heard to the girls. No one believed me. I couldn't fault them. So many times we had heard rumors, and they all fizzled out. Not a single soul dared to hope.

Only once did the bombs hit the factory. During one of the raids all the women were kneeling and praying to God to save us. Whereas unlike the others, I just turned to Zosia saying "Don't you dare to kneel and pray, it's better to look for the nearest window. If we get hit, we might be able to escape." The damage was slight and no one was hurt. Nevertheless, the Germans closed the factory. The track were destroyed, and the masters had no way to come to work.

Now, the Nazis became panicky. The very air seemed to be pervaded with their fear. They didn't care any more whether we knew it or not. We looked on as the once proud and mighty Germans were falling to pieces. They were hungry and scared, and we reveled in it. Of course, we did not let them see our joy. We were their slaves, and we were not sure what they might still do to us.

One night, the Kommandant woke us up and ordered the women to help the Russian prisoners to repair the destroyed rails. All the girls who worked in the factory were taken there, still under guard. They slaved the whole night and day, while the bombing continued all around. The girls told Mrs. Randowa that, no matter what reprisals would be taken, they would not return to the railroad track. When morning came, true to their word, they refused to go. The wardresses welcomed the rebellion. They, too, didn't like to go there but were afraid to disobey orders.

The commandant became livid. At first he threatened them with death, and when they stood firm, in desperation, he even begged. When this did not work he produced a letter, which had arrived that morning from the headquarters in Regensburg, with orders to take us to the forest and shoot all of us. Then he disclosed that, since the Russian army was within a few kilometers from us, he was not going to do anything so foolish. If we promised to help him when the Russians arrive, he would be willing to disobey his orders. Of course, we agreed. Satisfied, he left without making the women go.

Still, we didn't know what to expect. All the while, the kitchen was being emptied of what little food was left. What we had, we had to feed to the Germans first. As if this was not enough, along came a battalion of soldiers asking for a meal. The Kommandant ordered us to serve them. We had no choice: we had to part with our rations and the meal we were preparing for the guards. It was a sorry bunch at that, mere children, no more than twelve or thirteen years old. There was absolutely nothing left for us or any one else.

For the last time, we cleaned the kitchen, and, as we were ready to return to our quarters, the wardress Lisette asked me to remain. She escorted the girls, then came back. She said that she had a special job for me. She explained that close to our factory was a railroad station, and next to it was a post office depot. According to her, it was full of goodies. I was to break in and take whatever I needed. All she wanted was a pair of sturdy boots. She said that I had nothing to fear any more. The Germans were too busy worrying about the Russians. She would stay on watch, just in case.

We sneaked out the back door. I was petrified, yet I could not refuse; to me she was still my master. We walked in pitch darkness and came to the station. There wasn't a soul to be seen. We found the depot. Lisette had come prepared. She handed me a flashlight, picked up a stone, and broke a window. I climbed in and found the storeroom. There were huge crates marked men's shoes, boxes, suitcases; and many small packages addressed to soldiers, most likely mailed for sons or husbands. I don't recall how I managed to open most of them. Some were filled with fruitcakes and lots of wine bottles. While I searched for the boots, I gorged myself with cakes.

I kept opening box after box looking for shoes, then I came across a whole crate of ladies' boots. I whispered to Lisette to come in and try them for size. She climbed in through the same broken window I did. She found a pair that fit her perfectly and, to my surprise, she took only one pair. She wasn't interested in anything else.

I, on the other hand, felt like a child in a candy store. I stuffed a suitcase with cakes, wine, some sweaters, and raincoats. We returned to the plant the same way we left. I entered the living quarters, barely able to drag the heavy case. Two hundred women greeted us, cheered and listened, fascinated, as I related the whole escapade. The girls insisted that I take them there. They became bold and fearless. I was full of adrenalin and knew that I would not sleep that night. I had the flashlight, so we all ventured bravely out.

Once there, we took anything that wasn't nailed down. In no time, we stripped the whole warehouse clean. We dressed up and marched around like peacocks. We ate the cakes and drank lots of wine. We became tipsy. The commandant arrived; he ordered us to take everything back. The few Germans that were still there cried, repeating over and over, "Our poor sons and our poor fathers." We did give back some of the things, but not the raincoats, some sweaters, and the men's shoes—lots and lots of shoes.

I was still drunk. When I woke up, the cakes and wine, which I wasn't used to, took their toll. I felt ill. I went outside for fresh air and, surprisingly, saw no sign of any guards. I stood bewildered, and I thought that I was dreaming. After so many years of being a prisoner, it wasn't easy to feel free. I was still afraid. This was not real. What if the Nazis were planning a new trap; what would happen to us then?

Suddenly, I saw German civilians running somewhere. They were carrying pots filled with barley. Once more, hunger won over fear. I began to run with them. I followed the ones with empty pots. No one paid any attention to me. We came to a farm where a silo was filled with golden grain. The Germans were filling the pots. Since I didn't have one, I picked up my skirt and put as much as I could into it. I carried the barley back to the campgrounds. I went into the kitchen and handed it to an amazed Basia. She was very happy to have something to cook for the girls. Basia made the thickest soup ever. Then we carried it upstairs to the hungry girls.

This may sound unbelievable. The starving women could not eat it without any salt. Only Zosia, Mrs. Randowa, her daughter Helga, and I ate, thanks to the precious salt I organized from the storeroom.

28

Had I known that not much later we would be liberated, I would have shared it with all. But such was the way of life in the camps. You learned to be selfish. Now, since my belly was full, and I had found my freedom, I became even bolder. I went out once again. I don't know what I was looking for, but I found more than I expected. I was on a main road when I saw huge tanks and trucks, full of soldiers. Those men were throwing candy at the Germans and something else that I had never seen before. I picked it up and tried it. I was puzzled by that strange candy and didn't know whether I should eat that sweet, chewy mess or spit it out once the sweetness was gone. So I swallowed it.

Also, I was fascinated by those strange soldiers for they did not speak Russian but some foreign language I never heard before. They seemed to roll their tongues as they spoke. Next, I turned and pointed to the red stripe on the back of my coat. I became panicky when one of them grabbed me and put me on the tank. They didn't understand me, nor I them. All I could do is point them in the direction of the camp. Somehow, they knew what I meant and drove the way I was pointing. At first, the women thought that the Germans were returning to punish us, but when Mrs. Lernerowa was able to converse with these soldiers, she told us that those were Americans who came to free us.

She spoke perfect English. It seems that she and her family were to emigrate to the States, then the Nazis closed the borders. Consequently, she and her family were forced to remain, and like everybody else, they stayed in the Ghetto, only to be sent to the death camps, where she lost her husband and three children.

Learning that we were liberated, and that the liberators were not Russians but Americans, created lots of excitement among us. All I knew about the United States was that it was a new land full of cowboys and Indians and a lot of horse thieves—all this from the movies I saw in my uncle's theater.

Now those men were right here and, to our surprise, they were extremely nice, showering us with candies, saying nice things to us; not at all like those wild men toting guns and killing each other.

During the excitement that ensued, we didn't at first notice that the mean lame wardress was among us, wearing the same kind of uniform as us and, to add insult to injury, was making goo-goo eyes at them, claiming that she was one of us. It was lucky that Mrs. Lernerowa understood what she was saying. She then told our liberators the truth (the nerve of that bitch). They arrested her on the spot. Before they left, they gave us more chocolates and that strange candy they called chewing gum, which they chewed constantly. The girls bravely tried it and, to everyone's amazement, liked it. After the excitement, we became uneasy, even a little scared of those men in uniforms. We were not used to the kind of attention we were getting.

Soon the Americans returned. A captain who spoke German put us at ease. Indeed, we were free, he told us. That same evening, they fed us. We were given the same meal as the soldiers. We were surprised when we received a tray of meat, which they told us was turkey, and something sweet called cranberry, and, for the first time in two years, we ate with a fork and knife. We stuffed ourselves full. As a result of that banquet, the thirteen holes were constantly busy; we spent the whole night there. We became ill with diarrhea and terrible cramps. That lasted a few days, and we lost more weight in those two or three days than in the last month of starvation. The army medic came and forbade them to feed us with food from their mess hall. The Americans brought in German women, and ordered them to cook nothing but rice for the next few days. That was the only food we were allowed to eat. We recuperated slowly and regained our strength.

We were moved to a different place, some kind of warehouse. Across the street was a bank. We lost no time to take all the German money. Then we built a bonfire and danced around it.

A couple of days later, we were moved to a beautiful hotel in the mountains, where the German staff cooked and cleaned for us. One thing was missing; we had no clothes except the dirty uniforms. The American's took care of that. They confiscated uniforms from the German navy and presented them to us (these were the only small sizes they could find). We found a gramophone and records. Dressed as men, we played the music and danced, danced, danced.

29

One day, we were invited to an American soldiers' dance. They picked us up by truck; it was beautiful. They had a real band and a beverage they called coca-cola. The men were true gentlemen and treated us royally. There were some female soldiers were called WACS, and we were amazed by a dance called the jitterbug. Those women soldiers were dressed in spotless uniforms, while we were in our navy uniforms. I think that they thought that we were German navy women.

Every other week the soldiers held a dance, and we were always picked up for it. Once, coming back from such an evening, we heard shooting. We got scared; more so when the captain told us that those were German snipers who were holing out in the mountains. He warned us to be careful when outside and posted a watch at night.

Our life was great but at the same time uncertain. If one were to evaluate our existence in the first weeks after the liberation on the surface, one would presume that we had not a single worry. Not so. True, we lived in a hotel and had plenty of food, and we partied a lot. But underneath all that, we worried about our future. We wondered about our families. Were any of them alive? Would we ever find them, or are we the only survivors? Many nights I cried myself to sleep and heard Zosia sobbing also.

Once, we were admonished by the captain. It seemed that we had committed a big no-no. While hiking through some woods, we came across a group of Negro soldiers. Of course, to us it made no difference what their skin color was. Just the opposite; we were fascinated by them. Never before had we seen black men. We were anxious to learn the jitterbug, and they were happy to oblige. They were masters at it. Somehow the captain got wind of it. Consequently, we were given a long lecture and a stern warning not to do that again. We were bewildered. We could not comprehend this kind of discrimination. Were not those men Americans? And did not those men fight alongside the other soldiers? Was it different from the way the Nazis felt about us? And why were those men shunned? Those and many other questions troubled us a lot. Being accustomed to fear authority, we obeyed and stayed away from the black soldiers.

This incident reminded us how unfair discrimination was. We were asking ourselves what kind of a life we were to look forward to? We talked about it constantly. We began to question our liberators. We were extremely anxious to know what we could expect now that we were free. The captain brought a chaplain to explain things. He sympathized with us but had no reasonable explanation. All he told us was that everyone has to respect the law of the land. But then, did not the Germans respect the law against the Jews? Anyhow, he did have some good news for us. He came with a prepared list of camps and names of some survivors. Out of the two hundred women, only one found her husband's name on it. The chaplain made arrangements to bring him to the hotel. We all were excited and happy for her. The day the chaplain brought him to meet with his wife was jubilant and, at the same time, sad. It stirred a longing in all of us, a longing that we didn't expect to be fulfilled.

We watched from afar. It was the most important meeting we witnessed. I cried and laughed and felt a part of the reunion, as if it were someone close to me, perhaps a member of my own family that I yearned for.

30

Soon, we were preoccupied with other kinds of excitement. One by one, the girls were getting back their menses. With each one, we celebrated the return to normalcy. I discovered that my body was undergoing changes, to my delight. I was beginning to develop and grow breasts, and a short time later I, too, got my period. No longer was I a child. I was now a full-grown woman, the girls told me so.

At the same time, I became aware of the young men we met at the dances. I fell in love with a young soldier. His name was Tommy, and he hailed from a place called Texas. He would ask me to dance and sit by me at the table. The other soldiers called him a cradle robber. Soon they, too, looked at me differently—the power of breasts on a woman! Like many other things in my life, this innocent romance ended in tears. Tommy's battalion was sent to fight the Japanese. No more dances and no more boyfriends for any of us.

The new men stationed near us were a different breed from our liberators. They were new recruits that had not fought the Germans, were unaware of the camps, and didn't respect the "no fraternizing" orders. They didn't bother with us, the skinny looking girls. They preferred plump Frauleins.

Thinking back, I often wondered, were the German doctors the ones that developed a birth control pill and used it to experiment on us by putting it in our food? How else to account for lack of menstruation in the camps? Just a thought, perhaps a silly one, but worth contemplating. I would not put anything past the Nazis.

31

We continued to pester the chaplain about news from other camps. Were there many of them? If so, did some of the Jewish prisoners survive? It was a slow and chaotic process. We were told to be patient. Soon the allies would compile a credible list of survivors.

Meantime, we enjoyed whatever we were allowed to do. We visited the small villages and hiked into big towns. The German population was not too happy to see us walking through their streets. They used to close windows and doors and make believe we were not there. I'm sure that they resented us more than they feared us. We had no intension of harming them. But we had our own way of retaliate. For instance mad as we were we would take a crap right in front of their doors and then we would knock on the doors and ask politely for a piece of paper. Great fun.

Very strange. The Hungarian girls kept to themselves. Even Lola, did not socialize with us. We wondered why. Then came a day when we understood. It started one morning. The Kommandant showed up. Standing underneath Lola's window, he begged her to save him. It was pathetic. The once proud Nazi bastard imploring a Jewess to save him. After that comic performance, he was arrested by the Americans. Good. The next morning, the American CIA came. They questioned us about Lola and her checkered past. Since we knew nothing concrete, only rumors, we had little to tell them. The men had plenty to tell us. They intimated that Lola was wanted by every nation's criminal police, including the Russian NKVD. She was taken away under guard. That was the last time we saw her.

Every day, something new was happening. On a quiet afternoon, a man showed up. He claimed to be a Jew, traveling through Germany seeking family, hoping against hope to find someone, somewhere still alive. Sadness mingled with joy. A Jewish man alive, right in front of us. Our joy was mingled with sadness when he disclosed that, so far, he had not found anyone, but he would not abandon his search.

Meanwhile, drunk with freedom, we continued to hike into the neighboring towns. Once, while we walked down a street, we were surprised when we came across the mean wardress, the one with a limp. She greeted us as if we were long lost friends. We, who still wore the German navy uniforms, looked at her, not so much with hatered but with envy. She was dressed to kill—what Irony! Certainly, we didn't expect her to parade the streets free, much less to be so well off, and we didn't intend that to continue.

Some of us kept her talking, while a couple of women went to find the MPs. We had her arrested. We were unprepared for what happened next. Instead of incarcerating her, the Military Police brought her to us. We congregated around them. The women that were degraded, humiliated, and beaten by that animal were at a loss as to what kind of punishment to deal out. All we were capable of was shouting and spitting. Then one of the girls brought scissors and attempted to cut her tresses. One of the MP stepped in to protect her. We then vented our anger at him. Exasperated, he pulled out his gun and offered it to anyone willing to shoot her. All of us turned to the girl whose mother had been abused by her every single day. But she took her mother's arm and walked away. Amazed, we asked her why. She explained that she was not about to be brought down to the same level as the Nazis. End of story. There is not much I could add, except that we were not capable of committing cruelties.

32

Now that we had lots of time, we were constantly looking for excitement. Some of the soldiers would, at times, take us along on their forays. They needed people who understood and spoke German. We would enter a farm, take eggs and chickens, which we would give to the cooks, and have them make a healthy breakfast for us, while the soldiers would take all the valuables the Germans possessed.

One time, a couple of them told us about a large residence which was supposed to have a huge wine cellar and lots of jewelry. Zosia was excited. She dreamed of having a watch. Now would be her chance to get one. She insisted that we join the soldiers. We were reluctant. Most of the time, we knew the boys; this time we didn't. Nevertheless, we didn't want to disappoint Zosia, so just for the fun of it, we complied.

Upon arriving there, one of the soldiers suggested that Zosia go up with him to the master bedroom where, most likely, they kept the "Schmuck," jewelry in German. After they entered the room, the American pulled down his pants and exposed himself to poor Zosia, saying, "Here is the Schmuck!" Next we knew, Zosia came flying down the stairs, humiliated and scared but holding on to a watch she "organized." We all thought that it was funny, considering that it was the first and only time Zosia dared to do something brave. Instead of having fun, she had come across a crude ogre.

Then one day, we heard a rumor via a Hungarian girl, that in a nearby town (I don't remember the name), there lived a young Jewish boy, who according to that tale, wore an American uniform adorned with a stiletto and rode a bike. This imaginary boy was in charge of a warehouse full of materials. We longed for decent clothes. We had nothing better to do, so we decided to go there and seek out that strange creature.

There were nine of us, known as the daring bunch: Zosia's best friend Bella, the leader of our bunch; her sister Dincia; their cousins Adela, Itka, and Basia; Lola, the sister-in-law; Mama Novak; Zosia; and yours truly. We were the most adventurous "idiots." The town was fifteen kilometers away. In order of not to get lost, we decided to follow the track (trains were not operational). We marched in step, singing Jewish and Polish tunes.

We arrived late that evening. Hungry and exhausted, because of a curfew, we had to find a place immediately. After inquiring about a hotel, we were told that there was only one open to the public. Upon finding the inn, we asked for a couple of rooms for the night. The manager (also the proprietor), apparently a Nazi, refused, claiming that none were available. We were about to leave peacefully, when a chambermaid whispered to Bella that it was a brazen lie, for the hotel was practically empty. Bella returned to the front desk, demanding the rooms. Again she was refused. Zosia and Bella told the rest of us to stay put, while they went to fetch an MP. At that time, all you had to do was prove to the Americans that you were an ex-inmate of the death camps, and you would get all the help needed. The Americans were extremely sympathetic.

The girls returned, accompanied by two of them. They ordered the Nazi to give us lodging plus hot water for baths, and prepare an evening meal. Suddenly the rooms were there, and everything else also. After a nourishing dinner, a shower, and a good night's rest, we rose early and went to town looking for the boy on a bicycle.

The town was, in fact, only a small village. We had no trouble finding merchants who indeed knew the youth, but not his whereabouts. Excited, we roamed the narrow streets seeking the boy. By four in the late afternoon, we were ready to give up the quest. Just then, we spotted the elusive "prince". It must have been the most comical scene: nine girls, dressed in navy uniforms, chasing a youth, shouting, "Stop, stop, we came a long way to find you! We are Jews like you. Please, stop!" He must have heard us, for he stopped. He listened while we told him our tale of woe and why and how we got there.

He was a quiet soul, not very talkative. He just nodded, then he told us to follow him. Not too far away, we stopped and entered a building. Besides the stiletto, he carried a bunch of keys. He opened a door, and we were amazed to find a warehouse full of most beautiful silks and woolens. It was surreal. I felt like Alladin in the cave filled with treasures. Somewhere he found suitcases. He told us to fill them with whatever we chose. Like children in a candy store, we packed in as much as we possibly could, but then we could hardly lift them. He organized a child's wagon from a nearby yard. We piled the suitcases on the cart and again, because of curfew, we started on our way home.

During the hike, we talked and talked about our adventure and that we found a real Jewish boy alive. In our haste, we neglected to ask him where he came from or where he was during the war. It would have been crucial to know. Unfortunately we didn't, and most likely we would never see him again.

We arrived at the hotel late at night. Before going to sleep, we raided the kitchen. In the morning, excited, we split the booty. Between Zosia and me, we had enough to clothe a whole army.

Next, we found that a lot had happened while we were away. Again there was to be an upheaval in our lives.

33

Mrs. Randowa explained that while we were away, the captain told her that the American forces were ordered to withdraw from all of Saxony. This territory was to be occupied by the Russians within a few days. We had a choice to make. We could stay or we could go along with the Americans. Next, he said that he was in contact with the Allies; there was a possibility for us to emigrate to England or France. We decided to join the Americans and once again became the proverbial wandering Jews.

A day later, we packed whatever we had, including the record player (property of the hotel), the many pairs of men's patent leather shoes (from the post office), and the rolls of fabrics. A couple of days later, we were picked up by trucks and deposited at the railroad station, where, besides the soldiers who rode in Pullmans, there were the same old cattle trains for us. We boarded and soon were in motion. This time we were looking forward to a brand new life. A bright future, or so we thought. Unfortunately, the afore-mentioned countries didn't want us. The poor captain was at a loss as to what to do with us. We crisscrossed Germany, getting nowhere. Absolutely no one knew what to do with us. We were tired of the same old thing.

The convoy was making stops at various towns in order to pick up supplies. At one such stop, we were surprised to hear Hebrew being spoken by a couple of men who were loading the trains. Astounded, we jumped down and approached the men, who were also happy to learn that we were Jewish women. We told them as much as we could about ourselves. In turn, they told us that they were partisans who came out of hiding in the Polish forest upon hearing of the American liberators. Now they worked for the Red Cross. They lived in a town called Bamberg, and besides them, there were five more men—no Jewish women there. The men suggested that we get off the train and stay in Bamberg. They would help us to get settled, which, according to them, would be easy enough. Because we were for so long indoctrinated to fear authority, we were afraid of leaving the train without permission. Thus, we made arrangements for them to come at dusk, at which time we would make our escape. There were twelve of us in the boxcar, and all agreed to leave.

As planned, the men picked us up in a stolen jeep. They drove us into town. Here, too, was a curfew, so we had to hide in a doorway while the men and two of the girls (Bella and Zosia) drove to the American headquarters, where they would say that they found us wandering through Germany seeking lost relatives—a common occurrence. We waited, shivering from cold mingled with fear, while the MPs rode by looking for curfew breakers. Each second seemed to me an hour. Finally the girls came back, accompanied by three MPs.

We were squeezed into their cars and taken to an apartment that belonged to one of the Jewish men. The soldiers woke him up (he was sleeping with a Fraulein). The embarrassed man was told to allow us to stay there for the night. We slept on the floor, huddled together for warmth. We didn't mind it after the ordeal we just went through.

As soon as the sun came out, in came two high-ranking officers. They spoke perfect German. They were German Jews that, in nineteen thirty-eight, emigrated to America, and during the war, they volunteered to fight the Germans. The men took us to a beautiful house, property of the Burger Meister of Bamberg. He and his family were evicted, ordered to leave everything behind, and go with only the clothes on their backs.

We moved into that fully furnished home. The first thing I did was to look through the window, adorned by lovely lace curtains. I sat there, tears rolling down my cheeks. The girls had to practically pick me up in order to take me away from it. In the master bedroom, we found a drawer filled with women's garments. We now had panties, bras, and silk stockings. Every now and then I returned to the window. The women didn't understand my preoccupation with it and why afterwards, I sobbed.

We shared the three bedrooms, four girls to each; the master room we gave to mama Novak. Zosia, I, and two others slept in the only double bed with big European pillows and the softest feather comforter. The kitchen was big and contained beautiful china, which must have been taken from a rich Jewish home, the reason being that there were huge silver candelabras, the kind that Jews lit on holidays. Justice finally prevailed.

In the afternoon, a truck delivered crates of coffee, tea, sugar, flour, and lots of canned goods. The same evening, we were paid a visit by the two officers. We brewed tea, which we served in a silver tea set. In that relaxed atmosphere, we chatted about our experiences. They, in turn, told us about themselves. Because of their knowledge of the country and language, they were given the job of running the city of Bamberg. They promised to supply us with all we would needed. In return, we agreed that we would welcome any Jews that passed through the city. We were more than happy to oblige. From then on, we offered hospitality to the men and women who needed a place to rest and fed them too. From them, we learned that there were some survivors scattered all over Germany.

Since we were the first Jewish women in the city, news about us even reached the American soldiers. We were constantly visited by them who longed for a good Jewish meal. Some became steady customers. Every Saturday, we served a dish called chulent, a Jewish specialty.

Most of all, we waited for the weary travelers, ex-inmates of death camps, who possibly would have news about our lost relatives. Those poor souls always had some scraps of paper with names of people they came across. Each time we were disappointed, but we still hoped that maybe the next scrap of paper would have some good news for us. The days dragged on without the news we so badly needed, and the nights were painful. I tried not to think about my loved ones, afraid to hope. Every time we looked at those pieces of paper was a tremendous letdown. On many nights I heard some girl cry out in the sleep we all had.

One day, a young Jewish man showed up. He stood in our backyard shouting, "Amhu," which in Hebrew meant "the folk." Joyfully, we invited him in and let him bathe and rest. Afterwards, we questioned him about his search. He said that unfortunately, he didn't find anyone, and that we were the first Jewish females he came across. He admitted that he was tired of wandering across unfriendly Germany and was ready to give up. We suggested that he stay with us. He was welcome to sleep on the sofa in the living room. Eagerly, he accepted our offer, so now we had a male boarder. Since he was the only male among us, we named him Roosevelt, after the president of the United States.

Now that Ben (aka) Roosevelt was with us, he wanted to make sure that we had plenty of fresh eggs and fresh milk. In order to get it from the nearby farms, he needed a bike. Since we had no money to buy one, Ben "organized" it. He spent a day repainting the bike a different color, so that no one would recognize the stolen bike. All was well, until one day, while leaving said bike in front of a store, someone else took it. Ben was heartbroken.

We had fun writing a daily newspaper, where we reported all the happenings each day. We also posted a schedule of activities; for instance, who would cook, clean, or wash dishes that day. I was in charge of the lost and found section. With so many women in the house, someone always was missing something. After Ben lost "his" bike, I wrote a funny article about it. The heading went something like this, "Missing a stolen bike. The owner of a bike, which he acquired by theft, is seeking the said wheels that some unscrupulous thief stole. Reward—two eggs and a bottle of milk." Sorry to report, no one claimed the reward.

With all the soldiers coming and going, our lovely German neighbors began to look at us suspiciously. They presumed that we ran a house of ill repute. We had a sign on our door, which proclaimed, "Hotel Stehnicht," (Hotel Do Not Stand) to which we added, "but lie down," referring to the weary, tired visitors we often had. The "nice" neighbors reported us to the police. They came, checked our home, and realized that it was all in fun.

If truth must be told, we were getting a little tired of entertaining all the army personnel. Ben extricated us from the predicament we were in. He printed a sign, which said, "Off limits to soldiers." We placed it on the door, resulting in fewer visitors.

Then there was a time when there was a loud knocking on the door. Mama Novak looked through the peephole and announced that it was some important officer. Bella opened the door, and in came a very handsome, well-dressed officer. He bent from the waist up and said, "I'm Leman!" We figured that it was some kind of greeting, so we copied the move and replied, "I'm Leman." He spoke no German or Jewish; thus, we couldn't converse a lot. He left soon after. Day after day he would come, carrying gifts. Each time we would repeat the same greeting, "I'm Leman!" One day he showed up, followed by a translator. After we greeted them, the translator began to laugh hysterically. Once he calmed down, he explained to us the phrase "I'm Leman" was nothing more than a way of introducing himself. Much later, we were told that his father was a well-known Governor of New York.

Often, we had fun, and we would laugh a lot, only to cry ourselves to sleep. Our everyday lives were surreal. Yes, we were free, and yes, we had everything. Yet underneath our merriment, there was a great sorrow and longing.

One time, we decided to give a party for one of the girls. It was her twenty-fifth birthday. We asked a few soldier friends to help us celebrate. The boys brought wine and beer. We baked a cake, played records, danced, and became inebriated. All was well, until the girl became hysterical. The pent-up sorrow came to the surface. She began to scream and cry. We couldn't quiet her down. We were at a loss as to what do for her. She called for her mother, father, and her siblings. Exasperated, we called for an ambulance.

Dincia stayed in the hospital overnight. She was given some kind of sedative; by morning she was calm enough to come home. That experience left us wondering who might be next. We all knew that while we were tranquil on the outside, inside we were volcanoes that could explode at any time. We were edgy and morbid. It's not true that no news is good news.

34

Often, I thought that maybe someone, somewhere, was thinking of me. Zosia suggested that the two of us should go "home" to Poland. She quoted my dad, who often said that if separated, we should meet at home. Little did he know what we would go through and see after being torn apart. I didn't feel that Poland was more a home to us than Germany. We argued constantly. After one such disagreement, Zosia said that she would go, with or without me. She began in earnest to make plans to leave.

About the time she was ready, two men came to our door. They told us stories about the Russian occupation of Poland. They were liberated from camps in Poland. There was no freedom, and what's more, the Poles were no better toward Jews than before. By sheer luck, they were able to leave the place. They did have some good news; they heard about a camp liberated by the British army, where supposedly they found twenty or thirty thousand Jews alive. That place was Bergen-Belzen. The men were on their way there.

Once Zosia heard about it, there was no way of stopping her. She would accompany the men in search of our family. The journey would be a hard one, and it would take a long time. They would have to hitchhike—there were no trains or any other transportation to get there. Zosia promised to return to Bamberg if she could not find anyone. After a night's rest, the men left, taking Zosia with them. It was the first time we parted. I was convinced that we would never find each other again. I was inconsolable. I cried that whole day. I was sure I would lose her as I had lost the rest of my loved ones. The women tried to cheer me up. For my sake, they carried on with preparations for the Sabbath. They even made me take part in entertaining our guests, the soldiers, who anxiously awaited the dinner we prepared.

Alone, without my dear Zosia, more and more my thoughts turned to my future. I became more and more irritable. I realized that we could not continue much longer to live in Germany, surrounded by hostile Germans, who were living their lives as if nothing out of the ordinary had happened. On the contrary, they resented our presence there, without trying to hide their animosity.

We voiced our fears to our American friends. They sympathized but explained that, unfortunately, America was not ready to let us in, what with the quota and resentment of allowing more Jews into the States. America was not prepared for such a drastic move. They were more than aware of our predicament. They would soon be discharged from the army and go home. We, on the other hand, had no home to return to. In short, no one wanted us. They suggested that the only way we could beat the restrictions was to wed an American, if only for the formality, but that seemed an unpalatable measure, so that solution was rejected by all of us.

It had been only a week since Zosia left. To me, it seemed a lifetime. I missed her tremendously. Her absence was unbearable; I felt so alone. I could not envision my life without my dear Zosia. She was all to me—mother, sister, and, above all, the one and only one I now had.

35

Life went on. The women were beginning to pair up, some with soldiers, some with stragglers that were arriving daily. Our President Ben, and Dincia became an item. The boys who helped us to settle in Bamberg were competing for my attention. I was not interested in them or any other man. All I could think of was seeing Zosia again. I didn't know how much longer I could stand her absence. Even at the worst periods of my life, I knew that I had someone to come back to, and I could not envision my life without her.

One day, when it was my time to wash the dishes after the evening meal, we heard a car stopping in front of our house. We waited, curious to see who it was that came to us in such a nice car. It was a young Jewish man. He said that he drove from Bergen-Belzen, where he met a girl. She told him about us. It turned out that one of the girls was his cousin. Imagine his happiness finding a cousin alive. He lost no time, anxious to reunite with a member of his family. It was a very touching reunion. They embraced, sobbing from happiness. We all cried. After they calmed down, he suddenly remembered that he had a letter addressed to me. At first I thought that it was a note from Zosia, but when I saw the handwriting, I went limp and fainted.

When I came to, I explained to the women that it was a shock to recognize the writing. It was my brother, Steve, who wrote it. He said that he and Helen had found each other. They were getting married. Irene and David were alive; they all met in Bergen-Belzen. From Zosia, they learned that I, too, had survived. Finding that Lola's cousin was going to fetch her, they asked him to bring me along. The girls went berserk. They began to smash the beautiful china I washed just minutes before. I was in a daze. I felt like I was dreaming, afraid that I would wake to a terrible disappointment. If it weren't for the girls, who were so happy for me and Lola, I would not be able to accept the fact that I did have some of my siblings alive, and waiting for me. Needless to say, that that night, no one slept.

In the morning, the women helped me pack my measly possessions (I was too excited). After tearful goodbyes, the three of us left. Lola's cousin Joseph drove furiously on the beautiful Autobahn, which was built by the sweat and blood of the inmates of the death camps. He knew the roads well, and where we could find lodgings for the night (we could not drive through the night because of the curfew). There was a Polish "enclave" not far from the highway, and if were lucky, we might get a room for the night. Upon getting there, Joseph made arrangements. We were to stay in a room whose owners were away for a couple of days. Exhausted, we lay down on the bunk beds, only to be awakened by very drunk men, accompanied by German girls. Surprised but not mad, and obviously not embarrassed, they proceeded to have sex with the girls, while we stayed awake giggling the rest of the night.

We resumed our journey early. It took only two days. The Bergen-Belzen we left behind was not the one we knew only a few months before. The English army found the camp full of cadavers; some half dead, and most of them afflicted with typhoid fever. In order to contain the spreading disease, which was decimating the inmates, they moved the remnants of the women to barracks that previously housed the Nazis. The original death camp they burned to the ground.

I know *no* language that contains the necessary words to convey the joy of meeting with my family. At the same time, we bewailed the loss of Mother, Dad, and Zenek.

My brothers and sister admitted that not in a million years would they look for me, knowing well that almost all of the children were put to death. Dear, dear Zosia was extremely happy for us. I felt very sorry for her. How disappointed she must have been not to find any of her own siblings. She so hoped that her brother David was alive. Steve had told her about meeting him on the infamous death march. He and my brother David asked him to join them, but her brother David would not leave his comrades. Besides, he was positive that he had a better chance of surviving if he stayed with the Germans that were in charge of the march. They would not harm him (or so he thought), since he used to entertain them with his musical talent. He played the piano and the accordion for them. Some time later on that march, they met up with David's friends. They told them that it was those same Germans who killed him.

We talked all that night, even told each other little stories about our lives in the camps. Steve and Helen were very sorry that I missed their wedding, which took place a day before I arrived. The newly married couple was promised a room of their own. In the meanwhile, they stayed with Helen's cousin and his wife. Irene's room was tiny, and she had five roommates. Zosia slept with her on a cot. Consequently, there was no bed for me. I slept on the floor. I didn't mind it at all, as long as we were together. David stayed with a friend he knew in the camp, who was nice enough to let him sleep there.

Bergen-Belsen was not able to absorb all the people that came daily looking for relatives. Anyone who was not a part of the original prisoners at the time of liberation was not entitled to meals, which were rationed by the English. Irene and her friends shared with Zosia and me the little food they had.

Steve and Helen announced that they were going on a "honeymoon." Since they had no place of their own, they were going to hitchhike to Hamburg, where some of Steve's friends lived in a cigarette factory converted into a hotel. They insisted that I go along. Thus it happened that I went with them on their honeymoon.

We hiked and rode whenever we got a ride. Mostly, we were picked up by truckers. Helen brought along food, which she saved for the trip. On the last leg of our journey, we rode in the back of a truck that carried peat. It began to rain. We not only got soaked but also filthy. We took it all in our stride and laughed ourselves silly. As long as we were free and together, nothing else mattered. Life is beautiful, especially when you are young.

Somewhere on the outskirts of Hamburg, we stopped at a house, which was designated for "the wandering Jew." We were not alone. There were a lot of others there, so we lay on the floor and rested. We did get breakfast, which consisted of bread with jam and very strong coffee, brewed the day before. As the saying goes, it could wake a corpse. Revived by that brew, we continued on to Hamburg.

In the late afternoon, we arrived at our destination and so missed the lunch, not a good thing to do. We would have to wait till dinner to get eats. Steve's friends were overjoyed to see us, especially Helen. They knew all about her, for in those dark days he used to tell them about the love of his life. It made them feel human to listen to a past and a normal life, and made each of the men dream their own dream.

While we ate dinner, the men were busy preparing a "honeymoon suite" for the married couple. The suite consisted of a corner in the sleeping quarters, where they hung some sheets for privacy. My accommodation was the floor next to an older lady (perhaps in her forties). I awoke to a commotion and loud laughing. I was too naïve to know why. I asked Helen what happened. She was embarrassed. Still, she explained that it was the first time they had a corner of their own to consummate their marriage.

The following day, we went sightseeing. We visited the Hamburg port and anything that was still standing, including the famous "Puffs," the red district where the prostitutes sat completely naked in windows. Men were the only ones allowed to enter; women were positively not welcome. Helen did not believe that such a place existed; she had to see it for herself. Against advice, she ventured in, only to be chased out. It was a funny scene to see her hat flying out, followed by Helen running out, scared to death of the women chasing her.

"Our honeymoon" was, for me, a twofold success. I had fun, learned a lot, and at the same time, I admired the race I belonged to. We proved to be a hardy and forgiving people. How else could we live among those that did so much harm to us, yet we didn't hate them enough to do them harm. We walked among them with our heads held high, knowing in our hearts that we shall never forget.

Soon after, we had to leave. Steve wanted to get back. He was hoping that in our absence, they found a room for them. One of Steve's friends owned a car, and he was nice enough to offer us a ride back. Of course, we accepted and rode back to Bergen-Belzen in style.

When we arrived, we found that Steve and Helen were still homeless. Thus, they continued living with Helen's cousins, Sadie and Henry. Henry was a big man, with a heart to match. I visited them often. The reason being that I was hungry and ashamed to tell Irene. My sister tried her best to feed the extra mouths she now had. Henry was fearless. Often he left the enclave, which was against the rules, and managed to organize food from the German farmers. Whenever I was there, they would feed me.

The English authorities didn't approve of those forays. They didn't like us to mingle with the outside world. Part of the camp was fenced off, where they kept a few hundred former Russian prisoners who were not willing to go back to Mother Russia. Therefore, the English separated them from not only us Jews but also from the Italians and Hungarians. It made no sense to me that the former allies were imprisoned, while former enemies roamed the enclave free and mingled with the Jewish girls. So much for fairness.

36

The Tommies, as the English were called, held dances. Some of the women were invited by their soldier friends. Irene and her best friends, Jenny and Hansi, were also asked. It was imperative to have as many of us there as possible, the reason being the food that was available to organize once we were inside.

Our clever girls improvised a way to get the rest of us in. Upon leaving the ballroom for "fresh air," the Tommy stamped the girls' wrists, then the girls would press them against our wrists. Thus, the rest gained entrance. Years later, we would laugh recalling how we fooled the mighty English.

Especially, there was a time when Hansi, who was born and raised in Berlin, learned to speak a little Polish. On one such evening, some of the British soldiers invited a few Polish army nurses. We were uncomfortable about "organizing" the food off our table in their presence. We tried to be careful for them not to see it. Hansi, who was not too bright, asked in her broken Polish, "Do we take the beer also?" Talk about embarrassment. The nurses looked amazed. Why would we take the food? What did they know about hunger? We had neither rights nor enough food under the English.

We did have a movie house. Every Sunday there was a new film, mostly American pictures. One Sunday, while we walked toward the theater, I saw a young man. He wore a backpack, which was not unusual. Many men and women were arriving daily, seeking relatives. Looking toward the man, I became mesmerized. Something about him looked familiar. He reminded me of Zenek, except that my brother was blond, while this young man had much darker hair. I turned to Irene, who was deep in conversation with Steve. I asked her to look at that young man. She glanced at him, turned to me and said, "Don't torture yourself or us. Every time you see a young man, you think it is Zenek. I'm sure he perished. You know well that his name wasn't on any list of survivors." By then, we had looked at many such rosters.

Yet, I could not take my off eyes him. As he came closer, I called his name. Then he began to run toward us. My brothers had not seen him in five years. When they left for Germany, he was a thirteen-year-old boy. They could not believe that was Zenek.

Oh, the joy of finding Zenek alive. It was a happy and touching day for all. Now we were together, the five of us, the envy of our friends and acquaintances. Most of them were alone bereft of their family, while here we were, five children who survived. Zenek told us all about his miraculous journey through the camps, but he refused to tell us anything about Dad. He became nervous, and we could see that it was too painful for him. So we stopped asking.

Since we did not dare to question Zenek about it, I decided to seek out a friend of Zenek's, who was with him and my father in the camp. It did not take me long to find him. I proceeded to ask him if he knew what had happened to father. He was surprised to hear that Zenek had not told us anything. He remembered the day when Father was killed very well. It was not a pretty end, for our father who was so full of love and hope for humanity. On that fateful morning Zenek was forced to go to work and leave Dad behind in the barracks. Dad was ill, that is why he stayed behind. Moshe, the young man, being the Stubendienst (housekeeper of the barracks) witnessed the drama of my father's tragic end. A brutal German guard decided to have some fun with the famous dance teacher. The Nazi brought in a record-player and ordered Dad to dance to the music. Over and over again they played the record while Father was dancing. That brutal act went on for hours until my father crumpled down on the cement floor completely exhausted and died.

I have never had the heart to tell my brothers and my sister the tragic circumstances of our father's demise.

Zenek told us about his return to Poland. His first stop, in Lodz, was to go to Aunt Pola. A huge mistake. Zenek had no intention of asking her about the jewelry or anything else Mother gave her for safekeeping. What he expected was to be warmly welcomed, like a lost child. Instead of sympathy, she became upset and agitated. The first thing she said to him was, "I have nothing left; the Germans took all of it." Zenek told her not to worry; he had not come to collect, and she should relax. He left Aunt Pola's home disillusioned and heartbroken. He expected more from Mom's best friend.

Zenek went to the Jewish Gmina, where they fed him and gave him civilian clothes and a room to live in. The next day, he went to the Russians in charge of Lodz. He explained to them about Dad's business and asked them for permission to reopen the club. The Russians allowed him to do so. He found some of the former employees and began to run the business.

Our apartment was occupied by some Poles. He did not want them to be evicted, so he rented a place near the club. The business flourished. He was making a lot of money. He planned to stay there. Maybe someone was alive and would come back to Poland. What he didn't expect was the threats from Polish anti-Semites. He began to get vicious notes, which were thrown through his windows. The notes threatened him with death if he did not leave. They stated that they didn't want Jews in Poland.

He packed his belongings, took the money he earned, and left his homeland. After surviving the camps, he didn't want to be killed by Poles. He then wandered from town to town, seeking, asking, and looking. In one place, he came across a man who told him about Bergen-Belzen. Zenek decided to go there. He had a hard time getting out of Communist Poland. Because he had money and whiskey, he was able to bribe the Russian guards and entered Germany. Finally, he arrived in Bergen-Belzen and the rest is history.

Then I told him that it was Zosia, the gentle soul, who was instrumental in getting us together. I told him what Steve said about not looking for me, knowing the fate of the children. They were convinced that it would have been useless. We were so lucky. Our family was now complete, with the exception of our dear parents.

I must admit that my happiness was marred by the sadness I felt for my dear, dear Zosia. I was so very sorry and brokenhearted that she was alone, without her beautiful sisters and her handsome brother David. All of them were cut down in the prime of life. How she must have grieved. Yet she hid her pain, not wanting to spoil our joy and happiness. I vowed to myself that no matter what or where my life would take me, Zosia would always remain my most beloved sister.

37

In Bergen-Belzen, life was getting unbearable. The influx of many new wanderers forced the authorities to cut the food. We were literally as hungry as in the camps, and people were beginning to resent the fact that we were still kept behind barbed wires. We were not allowed to leave the grounds of the enclave.

We staged a demonstration demanding more from the English. They answered our demands with tanks and firing into the air.

I could not accept the way we were treated. More and more, I longed for the Americans, who were more than kind to us. I tried to convince my family to escape from Bergen-Belsen and settle in the American Zone. Zosia hesitated to make the move. She liked the idea of being in a place where so many Jews gathered, rather then living in a German town, where the Nazis still resented us. My siblings never really knew the freedom that I experienced. They were afraid of taking a chance of being on their own. Too many years we were taken care of, and they lacked the experience I had with the way the Yankees treated survivors.

I was invited to a gathering of young people. They seemed to be more aware of the world outside Bergen-Belsen. I was especially taken by one fellow. He spoke passionately about the Americans and even more so about Palestine, which he called Israel. Frankly speaking, I knew very little about Zion. He, on the other hand, knew a lot and called it our future home. I was told that he worked and lived in Frankfurt, where he was employed as a secretary to General Eisenhower. He was a Sabra, born in Palestine. He and his parents were visiting family in Poland and were caught in the middle of the turmoil that ended with the war. Consequently, they suffered the same fate that befell all. He lost both his parents. He felt a kinship with the remnants of our people. He spoke to us and made us think of a future in Israel. I was smitten and fell madly in love.

I was aware that he noticed me and looked in my direction when he spoke. Afterwards, he offered to take me home. When the meeting was over, he drove me on his motorcycle to the place I called home. He kissed me goodnight. This was literally the first kiss for me. I felt like fainting. My heart fluttered; my knees seemed to be made out of rubber. I never knew that love could be such an overwhelming feeling. Before he left, he told me that he was leaving in the morning for Frankfurt. He assured me that he'd back soon.

The next week, Steve's friend Karl was getting married to his lovely girlfriend, Sadie. The wedding was taking place in one off the mess halls. All of us were invited. After "Palestinczik" left, I was moping the whole week, and I was in no mood to attend. Irene and Zosia insisted that I go. Reluctantly I went along. I had spent that whole week expecting him. When he didn't come, I was tremendously disappointed. It didn't help when Zosia and Irene where teasing me about Palestinczik. The mood was festive; the band played. Steve was playing the drums, and everyone was dancing, the terrible years of suffering forgotten for the moment. Joy of life took over. Everyone was happy except me. I sat in a corner of the room, thinking of Abramek (his real name).

One of the girls I met at the meeting came over to chat. During the conversation, she mentioned that she came across Abramek. She said that he seemed to be preoccupied, looking for someone. At that moment, I felt that I would burst from excitement. Of course, I didn't say anything. I was sure that he was looking for me. If he was back, I thought that he should have come to see me. He knew where I lived. My pride was hurt. I could not understand why he didn't. Lusia kept on and on. I didn't hear what she was saying. My heart beat so loud that I was afraid she might hear it. I wished that she would leave. I decided to go home. I told her that I didn't feel well and had to go. I hurried for the exit. Suddenly I felt a hand on my shoulder. I turned and found myself looking straight into Abramek's eyes.

He took my hand and led me back to the mess hall. We sat down. He proceeded to say how much he missed me and could not stop thinking of me. He had a plan. He would find a nice place for me and my family in Frankfurt. He would also supply us with everything we needed. He made me promise that I would propose it to my family. We remained at the wedding until it broke up and the guests began to leave. Abramek walked me back to our "spacious" quarters. At the last minute, he decided to join me and my family. He then informed my siblings about the plan. To my surprise, he convinced them that it would be a good move for all of us.

But not all were enthusiastic about it. Steve and Helen were reluctant to make the move. Helen was pregnant. They were seriously thinking about leaving Germany altogether. Both agreed not to have the baby in that miserable country that did so much harm to our people, if they could only help it. Unfortunately, it would take more than eight months for them to get that promised visa from Helen's uncle in America. Meanwhile, they would try to get into Belgium. At the time we were to leave, David backed out. He fell in love with Jenny and would not leave her behind. Zenek agreed to go wherever we went. Abramek said that it would not take longer then a week to find appropriate living quarters. I could not have been more elated. Finally I would be with the love of my life and in the American Zone

Abramek promised to send a car to fetch us. Because he worked for the Americans, he had access to a lot of resources. We should not worry; he would work it all out. True to his promise, he did send a limousine for us within a few days. He was just as anxious to have me there as I was to be with him. Besides, I was really glad to leave Bergen-Belzen. We had no problem fitting our possessions in the car; we had so very little. We said our goodbyes to the few friends we had, and we were on our merry way.

Riding in style in the car, we arrived in Frankfurt the next morning (no more curfews for us). Abramek was waiting for us anxiously; he could not wait to show us the house we were now to live in. It was a very spacious place, beautifully furnished with five bedrooms, but there was a catch to it. The Germans who owned the house would live with us. The lady of the house would be cook and housekeeper. Her husband would not be in our way, since he was badly incapacitated by the war. He would stay in his room at all times. She seemed nice and couldn't stop saying how badly she felt about the way her people treated us. She then insisted that we call her "Mutti"—"mother" in German.

38

We settled in. For the first time since liberation, Irene had a private room and all the conveniences—a spacious bed and plenty of food. Zenek loved that place; he too had a room all to himself.

After a few days, Irene, Zosia, and Zenek found out that there was a displaced person's camp in a nearby town called Zelcheim. Every morning the three of them would go there. Irene got a job taking care of war orphans. Those children that had been left with Christians were now gathered by Jewish soldiers called Haganah. They knew absolutely nothing about their Jewish roots.

Most of those children were indoctrinated by their Polish keepers to hate Jews. Consequently, they were hostile and unhappy to find that they were Jews. They had to be "brainwashed." It was a hard task to bring them back to their heritage. Zosia, too, found employment. She became a hostess in the mess hall, which also substituted as a ballroom, where the young men and women worked out their energies and frustrations trying to enjoy life, which for so many years was denied them. Zenek also got a job in the American PX.

Abramek had to work every day, so I was left alone with nothing to do but wait for him to come home. When he did, he was too tired to do anything. Because the displaced camp was blossoming into a Jewish town within a town, the three of them would often stay overnight. When they did come home, they would tell me about the life there, the many people they met. Jews from all of Europe, now homeless, gathered there.

My life in that house was becoming more and more like a golden cage. I, too, was yearning to get out and have some fun, but it was not to be. Abramek was content just being with me, whereas I ached to spend time with the young people at the displaced persons camp. Whenever I suggested that we should go there, if only for a weekend when they held dances, he would become upset with me. He had no time for such trivialities and could not abide the idea that Jewish youth was preoccupied with fun, while people in Palestine lived under English mandate. Instead of dancing on the cursed German soil, they should yearn to go to the Promised Land to fight for its freedom and be done with the English yoke. Never mind that there was no legal way to get there. He would then explain that there were other means of getting there, with the help of Haganah."

In the meantime, I longed to have a good time. I begged Irene to take me along, if only once in a while. She refused, saying that it would not be right for me to go without Abramek, who was so generous to us. Despite the rationality of it, I was more and more restless each passing day.

"Mutti" sensed my loneliness. She was afraid that I would fly the coop, and she would lose a good thing (the goodies she received). In true German fashion, she tried hard to put me and Abramek into one bed, but I wasn't ready, and he was too old fashioned to take advantage of the situation. Frustrated, she began to invite her cronies with their daughters for company. I was not about to make friends with the Nazis' offspring. One of her guests was her own sister in-law with her brat. It proved to be Mutti's undoing.

One afternoon when Mutti was out shopping, the sister-in-law visited me. Jealous of the goodies that Mutti shared with us (chocolate, coffee and cigarettes)—things that were scarce and practically impossible for Germans to acquire—she proceeded to tell me the truth about Mutti and her supposedly ill husband, who was bedridden as a result of the terrible wounds he suffered while in the war. In fact, he and their son, who was in a Russian prisoner of war camp and of whom she never spoke (in fact, we never knew he existed)—both father and son were the city's most renowned Nazis. The son was imprisoned for atrocities he committed while working in a concentration camp, the same one in which his father was a commandant. Now he was afraid to show himself, lest someone recognize him. The nice lady brought a photo album with her to prove those allegations. I became sick to my stomach. So much for German family loyalties. I looked at the pictures and felt nauseous, and I threw up. This was a women that repeated over and over again how much she was sorry and how badly she felt for us; she even insisted that we call her "Mutti." By the time Abramek came home, I was shaking with rage. I told him that I could not stay there a minute longer. Abramek realized that there was nothing he could do or say to stop me from leaving. He insisted that I remain for the night; besides, there was no way to get to the camp so late at night.

I left early in the morning. I took a trolley to the next town; from there I found a truck, which was owned by two enterprising Jewish brothers, and which substituted for a taxi. On the way to the displaced camp, they told me that the place was overcrowded and that it would be impossible to get a room. They offered to let me stay with them until I find someplace to bunk. I thought that it was nice of them. I said so and I thanked them. I explained that I had family there and I was sure to be able to stay with them.

At the camp, I inquired where I could find the orphanage, but no one new much about it, much less where it was located. I decided to stop at the police station. Dragging my suitcase, I walked there. It was a long way, but I made it. To my surprise, there were many others waiting to be accommodated. I could not believe my eyes when, among them, I found two of my camp sisters from Bamberg, sisters Itka and Adela. The unexpected meeting was joyful. We spoke of the many things that happened to us since the time we parted.

While we were chit-chatting, a Jewish policeman approached, stating that unfortunately there were no rooms available, but that he would be glad to let us bunk in his place while he was on duty for at least a couple of nights. He also told us that there was only one bed there (what else was new?). We were welcome to it. Graciously we accepted, and he walked us there. The room was so sparsely furnished; one table and a couple of rickety chairs and a chest of drawers. The bedding was something else; typically European, with big pillows and a great down comforter.

The three of us laid on the one bed, talked a little more and rested. After a while we got up, left our meager possessions, and ventured out. I found the orphanage and surprised Irene. She was mad at me for leaving Abramek. I explained and told her about the things I found out about "Mutti" and her family. She understood the reason for my flight and agreed that I had to leave that "home." Irene was pleased that we got a room for a couple of days; it would give her time to find a room for her and me. She had no place of her own but stayed with a friend, a male friend, one she knew in the ghetto. Zosia was sharing a bed with a female friend, and Zenek slept on the floor in the same room. So much for my expectations for staying with them.

Next, we went to see Zosia. She was elated to see me and the girls from Bamberg. After gossiping for a while about the rest of the girls, she told us about the evening dance. It was being held in a room that had a piano and a stone floor. It made no difference; we were anxious to attend. We were hungry. I had not eaten since that morning. Zosia fed us; she had plenty of food in the room, food that she brought from the kitchen where she worked.

The dance would not start until nine, so we had time to look around the camp. Zosia took us on a tour. Zelcheim was a small village with manicured lawns and little gardens; very "Gemutlich," as the Germans were fond of saying. The American authorities confiscated some of the houses, resettled the owners, and assigned them to the homeless refugees. Thus a "Shtetel" was born.

Anxious to go to the dance, we left early, but by the time we got there, the place was almost full. So we made a grand entrance. Itka and I wore the same dresses, which a seamstress in Bamberg fashioned from the same cloth that we acquired from the boy with the stiletto. We entered, and all heads turned. Perhaps they thought that we were twins, or maybe it was because we were the youngest and the best-looking girls there. We were surrounded by practically all the men who were present, and I was basking in the attention from men, old and young alike. I danced the whole evening, and I was a very proficient dancer. After all, my dad was my teacher, and I remembered it well. I was the belle of the "ball." Abramek all but forgotten, it felt good to be free and careless.

I flirted with the good-looking boys and was terribly flattered when one particular handsome young man had asked me to be his girl. His name was Edward, and he was a policeman. He really looked dashing in the uniform. He was quite enamored with me, and I was basking in the attention. I must say that I, too, was taken by him. Zosia tried to warn me, saying that he had a reputation among the women of Zalcheim. Nevertheless, after that evening, we became an item. People were saying that we were the most beautiful pair on the campgrounds. At first, I felt a little guilty when I thought about Abramek and all he did for me and my family. If truth must be told, I felt extremely bored with him and his serious outlook on life. All I wanted was to feel young and enjoy life.

Soon we had to vacate the room we stayed in. We still had no place to call our own. Itka and Adele decided to go back to Bamberg, where they had that nice home. I was sorry to see them go. Now I was on my own and once again homeless. One of the girls I befriended gracefully offered to share her flat. I eagerly accepted. Thus, we became roommates.

After I was settled, Dave and Jenny arrived. They too had nowhere to live. We gathered our clan and marched into the office of the president. We persuaded him and the people in charge of housing to let us have a house where the whole family could reside under one roof.

The next day, they let us have a small house in which a single German woman lived. The Americans took charge of it and resettled her. The home had three bedrooms, which was more than adequate for us—two upstairs and one on the main floor—and a huge kitchen that doubled for a dining and living room. There was a bathroom with a tub, a shower, and a toilet. There was also a storage room, which we agreed to let a couple of young women share with us. Irene and her friend Paul planned to marry; thus, we gave them one of the rooms upstairs. Zosia, our friend Hansi, Zenek, and I occupied the other bedroom. David and Jenny opted for the one downstairs. No one minded that they lived together, especially when they also planned to wed. In the back of the house was a nice little garden, where the previous owner planted vegetables. In exchange for letting her harvest them, she agreed to do house work, which suited us well.

The town had a little schoolhouse, which I attended religiously. I was hungry to learn all I could. Afterwards, I helped Irene at the orphanage. I did whatever was needed. Mostly I played with the little ones, especially the children that didn't want to be Jewish.

One of the saddest cases we came across was a little tot, perhaps four or five years old. His parents, not having any one to leave him with, left him on a dirt road in the Ukraine. They preferred to take that chance for their six-month infant, rather than having him exterminated in a camp.

The father survived. He immediately went looking for the child, searching and hoping that the little one was saved by someone who would take pity on the baby. He found him. The boy was living in a barn with only a cow for company. The farmers that found him raised the child to be a shepherd. The poor little waif had never been spoken to. He had learned no human speech; the only sounds he uttered were similar to ones the cow made. In the orphanage, he was given speech therapy. When he finally learned to talk, he constantly asked for his cow. He missed it a lot, more so than the farmers that brought him up missed him. He was a very sad little shepherd.

There were many such little lost souls that were daily brought to the orphanage. Irene worked diligently with them. She even brought some of them home, in order to make them used to a semblance of family life.

39

Zelcheim was gradually taking shape. Eventually, most of the Germans left the village, so we had it to ourselves. Fewer and fewer newcomers were arriving. The people in charge were doing a good job. We were given necessities, and we settled in comfortably.

Human nature is such that once it has all the most urgent needs satisfied, it strives for more. In order to achieve it, the men began to barter. From the American soldiers they bought cigarettes, coffee, chocolates, and other things the Germans were fond of but could not get those things in postwar Germany. The Yankees knew it well and supplied them to our boys at inflated prices.

At first, the men would sell the goods and exchange them for meats or poultry, which we didn't get. Soon they would barter for gold, watches, and other jewelry pieces, knowing well that some of it was most likely taken from us. Then the men and women became fashion conscious. Many of the men were tailors and shoemakers. For a price, they would make beautiful suits and leather boots in the latest styles. The American authorities called it a black market, knowing well that without the Yankee soldiers that supplied the goods, there would not be a "black market."

The ladies, in the meanwhile, began to grade the eligible men by points. If one had a leather coat, a motorcycle, a "shtopper" (a watch), or a dog, he would be graded as the most wealthy and desired one. Such a man could get almost any girl he wanted. More women had perished; thus, the men were constantly competing for the ladies. Once a girl was won, she not only got a husband but a good provider as well. Consequently, there was a rash of marriages. Much later, we coined a saying that "Hitler was the matchmaker," and many a bride was with child while standing under the "hupah." The more affluent ones had very elaborate weddings, which were held in the beer hall. Others were married in the mess hall. That year I attended more nuptials than in the rest of my life.

From the UNRA, a Jewish charity organization, I received two dresses. The distribution of clothes was not unlike the camps. One was given the articles, whether they fitted or not. One of the dresses was a very pretty black wool, which needed only a little a fixing. The other one was a baroque maroon gown made for a large person. I traded it with an older bride for a small navy blue coat. In lieu of shoes, which I needed badly, I was given a pair of baby booties. When I complained, I was told to trade them with someone who was expecting an infant. The rest of my wardrobe consisted of skirts I sewed myself, using discarded trousers that Zenek and Paul gave me. I also fashioned blouses from their old and torn shirts.

Zenek and Paul began to trade on the black market. At first Zenek, Zosia, and I would receive a chocolate once a week, which we gave to them. Slowly, they too developed "clients." Soon they were doing well enough, and our family was well provided with necessities.

Irene and Paul could now have a nice wedding. They got married a week before David and Jenny. We cooked and baked food for the receptions, which were attended by most of the friends we made in Zelcheim.

David was working as a policeman. He had no stomach for trading with Germans. One night, while on duty, he came across a farmer with a truck loaded full of cows and pigs. The man was looking for someone to sell them to. David lost no time in introducing him to Paul, who bought the whole load. During that night, we pushed the cattle and pigs down into the basement. In the morning, Paul went in search for butchers. He found a couple who were willing to slaughter them, but they couldn't settle on a price. While he was looking for others, the livestock were losing weight by the hour, and one of the sows gave birth prematurely (we didn't know that she was pregnant). She had eight and all but one died. We took the infant upstairs and nursed it with a bottle of milk we got from the cows. The piglet thrived extremely well. We became fond of it and, dressed it in little a little dress Jenny made.

We really weren't expecting any visitors. Nevertheless, we got some. Unfortunately, it was the German and American police. It seems that someone told them about our livestock and the inquiry Paul made about a professional butcher. They advised us that it was unlawful to slaughter animals for trade. At first we denied even having livestock, while the cows mooed and the pigs squealed. It sounded like some grotesque opera. In the end, we had to admit that indeed we had the animals. We showed them the basement where we kept the herd. They were just about to confiscate them, when Jenny, with her penchant for comedy, brought down the dressed little piggy, explaining that we raised the whole herd from infancy and that we considered them pets. After the laughs died down, the uniformed men left empty handed.

Paul gave in to the butcher's demands. As it was, he lost more money by holding out. The animals lost a lot of weight. The men did the job, killing all but the little piglet. We had become quite fond of it and raised it to maturity. Eventually, we placed it on a farm.

40

I was having the best time of my life. Edek proved to be a very attentive boyfriend. We went all over the city of Frankfurt on his motorbike. Most often, we went to the zoo, where the Germans had a band playing and there was dancing. We would meet our friends there. We didn't mingle with the Germans, and we would sit at a table far away from them. It was really more like a cabaret than a zoo.

One evening, a group of Nazis' descendants sat down at an adjoining table. They were dressed in some kind of a uniform on which there were some initials. Zenek inquired about those letters. Without batting an eye, they explained that they stood for Young Germans Are Needed By Hitler. Enraged, our boys attacked them. A fight ensued. I must admit that our boys did an excellent job. Someone called the cops. Suspecting that their sentiments would be on the side of the German youths, we made a run for it. Luckily, we left before the police arrived.

Abramek heard about the melee. Early the next morning, he showed up. Poor Abramek. He still considered me his girlfriend, and he became agitated. He admonished me for being there in the first place and for running around with wild and stupid teens. I was speechless. Many times, I tried to tell him that somehow I didn't feel the same way as he anymore, but Abramek wouldn't accept it. He surprised all of us when he asked Irene and Paul for my hand in marriage. He would take me to Sweden, where his uncle was a political official. From there, we would legally emigrate to Palestine, where he was a citizen. My family was all for it. They would be pleased to see me married and away from Germany. Of course, I could not agree. My life was just beginning. I would not give up my newly found freedom. Besides, by then I was infatuated with Edek, who was such fun, while Abramek was much too serious.

I was proud and happy when heads were turning as Edek and I walked or rode the streets of Zalcheim. Edek was six feet tall and had the most gorgeous blue eyes and blond, wavy hair. I, myself, was often told by men and women alike that I was the prettiest girl in the enclave, even stunning. They called me the sunshine of the camp.

I cried and felt very, very guilty when Abramek left, rejected by me and broken hearted. Soon after, I heard that he left for Palestine.

In the 1948 war with the Arabs he died fighting for his beloved country.

41

I learned that nothing in my life was constant. The Israeli Haganah became very active, convincing the youth that, regardless of the perils, our best answer to the situation we found ourselves in was to emigrate to Israel and fight for a country of our own.

We realized that no one wanted us, including the perpetrators who were responsible for our plight. We began to hold Zionist meetings sponsored by the Haganah. Soon, most of my friends began to leave for Israel. Since there was no legal way to enter it, they were smuggled in old rickety boats, assisted by Jewish organizations, which sprang up all over Europe despite the fact that it was dangerous to make those sea voyages. Jewish youth was filled with idealism and they were willing to get there any which way they could.

My boyfriend announced that he, too, was leaving. He would get to Israel via Italy and asked me to join him. I was excited and agreed to accompany him. Because I was underage, Irene, as my guardian, was ordered to sign a permission paper. She flatly refused. No amount of pleading helped. She stood steadfast. It was for my own good, she explained. She felt that I suffered enough for five years, and going to a war-torn country would be too much. She wanted me to have a normal life—a place where I would have a chance for a peaceful and decent existence.

Zelchaim became a lonely and quiet town. With so many young people gone, I became depressed; especially so after Edek left. And to make things worse, the Haganah took the children from the orphanage for Israel. Irene was now idle, but because she was with child, she enjoyed not having to work with those pitiful lost little souls. I was completely unaware that she was quietly conspiring with an American social worker to get me to the United States.

Irene had met Mrs. Roosevelt, the wife of the president, while that gracious lady visited the orphanage. At that time, she heard that the lady was planning to "adopt" five hundred teens from the displaced camps. The social worker assured Irene that she could arrange for me to be one of those children. My sister was overjoyed, and the two of them began to make the necessary plans for me to meet the lady.

Soon after, I was called to Frankfurt, where I met with her secretary. She made all the necessary papers and assured me that I would emigrate to the States. In the meantime, we received news from Steve and Helen. They left Bergen-Belsen to be smuggled into Belgium and were caught on the border, where they were detained in prison. Luckily, they met a chaplain, who found a distant cousin of our dad's who was willing to sponsor them. Their wish came true, and their little boy was born in Brussels, Belgium.

Zosia met a nice man and fell head over heels in love. I was happy for her and glad that she had someone to call her own. She spent most of her free time with her lover. I must admit that I missed having her to talk to. The two of us had a special bond that no one else had with us.

Zenek also was too busy for me. Besides his work, he now had a lady friend. He was dating a much older German woman. We were not happy about that May-December liaison; more so because she was German. We decided not to fight it, hoping that it would take its course and he would come to his senses.

David and Jenny also decided to try to get into Belgium. They, too, hired a smuggler. Now I found myself alone and bored. I began to write poetry, and I must say that it was quite good. Anything to keep busy helped. Those of my friends that decided not to go to Palestine left for any country that would allow them to settle in.

Just when I felt desperate, I was called to the American consul. I was to meet with Mrs. Roosevelt. The lady was nice and easy to talk to. We spoke with the help of a translator. During the interview, it dawned on me that I would be completely alone in a foreign country and far away from the people I loved. I was very scared, and I began to cry. Mrs. Roosevelt was taken aback. I'm sure that she expected me to be ecstatic; instead, I was sobbing uncontrollably. She began to question me. I told her why I was afraid and reluctant to leave my family, after five years of being alone, separated from all I loved. I spoke about the way we met after the liberation and how miraculous it was, finding all my siblings, while others like my cousin, Zosia, were left alone; and that by going to the States, I would be on my own once more. If only I could be with one of my brothers, who was the only one still single. Then that gracious lady asked, would I be happy if he was with me? She asked how old Zenek was. I told her that he was only two years older than I (actually, he was four years older). Her eyes lit up. She explained that it would be possible, if she changed his age and made him younger, then he, too, could be adopted by her. I liked that and thanked her. I left for home elated and excited. Now Zenek and I would go to America together.

But Zenek was skeptical about the possibility that he could pass as a minor. His take on the whole episode was that Mrs. Roosevelt was just being clever in order to get me to emigrate to the States. I believed her, so he could not convince me otherwise. She was too nice to lie, and I wanted him to be just as excited as I was. We were going and there were to be no ifs or buts.

In the meantime, my brother was having a good time with his lady friend. She showered him with gifts—her husband's possessions—including a motorcycle, most likely taken from some young man in Europe. She gave him a gold watch and men's silk shirts from France. She kept him busy, and in a way, happy.

We accepted the situation, for it happened at a critical time for Zenek. He and his coworkers were let go from their jobs. It was as a result of a stupid prank the boys played on the soldiers. They mixed some salt with sugar at the mess hall. They meant no harm, but the Americans acted as if it were sabotage.

Ever since the terrible day when the Nazis took Mom away, Zenek suffered from melancholy. At times, he was suicidal. The slightest disappointment would set him off. We learned that, when we asked him about our father and the circumstance of his demise. Needless to say, we never again questioned him.

Much later, we did hear about it from a friend of Zenek's, who was there when it happened. The man revealed to us the terrible way our dad was killed. One of the Nazis somehow found out that Dad was a well-known dance teacher. That sadist made my dear dad dance for hours at a time, and once when Zenek was at work, Father was forced to perform for those animals. He danced and danced until he fainted. Bored, the Nazi shot him while he lay there exhausted. When Zenek came back, Father was gone, and when he questioned his camp brothers, they told him the sad truth. The rest of my life, I tried to erase my memories of the bestiality perpetrated by that well-educated, highly regarded nation. Will I be ever able to forget? Forgive? I don't think so.

42

As we expected, Zenek tired of the German woman. He tried to extricate himself in a nice way. He offered to return the gifts. Still the "lady" would not let go. He decided to leave Frankfurt for a while. He went to Munich, where he had a friend. While there, he came across a band of Gypsies. They had brand new cars for sale at bargain prices. Zenek came back all excited about the deal; he and Paul bought the cars. They had no problem selling them on the black market. In fact, they made a big profit. Zenek bought one for himself. Everyone was awed by that deal except me. I had a bad feeling about it and did not hesitate to say so. My argument was that even Jews, who were excellent traders, could not possibly put anything over the Gypsies, and I was sure that there was a reason those people sold the cars at such a low price. Sorry to say, I was right. The Americans proclaimed that it was unlawful for foreigners to own automobiles. It must have been a sting set up by the MPs, who were not averse to such deeds.

Because his ex-girlfriend still clung to him, Zenek decided to find his way into Belgium, where he would stay with Steve for a while, until the lady cooled off. Before he left, he gave the keys to the car to Paul for safekeeping. One day after he was gone, the military police showed up. They demanded the keys to the car, in order to confiscate it. Paul tried to tell them that it was not his; thus, he could not let them have the keys. The authorities became nasty. Irene, in her ninth month of pregnancy, became nervous. In Polish, she told Paul to surrender the keys to the vehicle. Paul, aggravated, retorted in Polish, "I will not. I'll give them shit," whereas, one of the MPs replied, "Shit you keep for yourself. The keys you'll give me." Astounded, Paul handed over the keys. The man opened the trunk. Still seething with anger, Paul went over to see if there was something personal of Zenek's there. The MP shoved him hard, and Paul almost fell into the trunk. Relentlessly, the policeman continued to push Paul. Paul grabbed a hammer from the trunk and, in self defense, hit the man over the head; fortunately, not hard enough to do him much damage. Nevertheless, it was considered a capital offense. Paul was arrested and led away as if he were a common criminal.

Irene became hysterical. She begged them to release him. She began to get contractions. I was afraid that she might give birth right then and there. The men thought that she was putting on an act. They laughed as they left with Paul in tow. It took only a few minutes to turn our lives into a nightmare once again.

I called the doctor, who gave her a sedative. He calmed me down, saying that she would be well after a while. I, too, was in shock. I felt violated by the injustice and never forgot that ugly incident.

The next morning, Irene, Zosia, and I went to the American police department. We hoped that they would consider the circumstance and release Paul, but to no avail. We returned home despondent. Justice undone.

I was summoned to the council, not knowing what to expect. Frankly, at that time I was more concerned about Irene than myself. Now I was full of doubts about fairness in the United States. At the council, a very nice man explained that Zenek and I would be sworn in, examined by a doctor, and soon after leave for America. This had to be completed in only three days.

I was in trouble again. Zenek was away, and I was afraid to admit that he had entered Belgium illegally. I was in a quandary. What was I to do? There was no way for me to get in touch with him. I didn't want to burden Irene with more problems than she already had. I asked a friend, who worked for the UNRA, if there were a possibility somehow to let Zenek know. The "friend" said that it would cost me. It would take five hundred American dollars to persuade the Yankee director to make the call. I didn't have any money, and I was not about to ask Irene for it. She had plenty on her plate without having to worry about my problems. Suddenly, I remembered that one of the German women Paul did business with lived in Cologne. That part of Germany was occupied by the Belgians. Could I possibly go there and maybe meet a nice enough soldier who would help me?

I had to tell Irene. I would need enough money to take a train to that city. Besides, I also needed that woman's address. We searched through Paul's papers, and sure enough we found it. The next thing I knew, I was on my way, armed with a carton of cigarettes and a few marks. I didn't even know if there was a train leaving for Cologne. If not, I would hitchhike there.

With the money Irene gave me, I took a taxi to the railroad station. I was in luck; there was a train going to that city within an hour. The only ticket available was in coach. I bought the ticket and waited to embark.

A young German male started a conversation with me. He asked if I lived there. I told him that I was going to visit someone. He noticed that I spoke with a foreign accent. He knew about the camps and was curious about my experiences as an inmate. I really was not in a mood to talk to this stranger about it and what's more, to a German, but he seemed to be genuinely interested in the death camps. He said that none of the people he knew would talk about them and that he would like to learn what really took place.

I didn't feel antagonism toward a young, innocent German. We spoke for a while. I told him some of my life while imprisoned, and he was really shocked. He also said that he'd spread the truth to his friends at the university. He offered to give me his first class ticket. I refused his generosity, saying, "No, thank you." He insisted that I take it, explaining that he was not going all the way to Cologne but to a nearby village where he lived. He also told me that the train would not go directly to Cologne. The station there was in ruins. It would leave me off on the outskirts of town, and I would have to walk the rest of the way. I would also have to cross a temporary bridge, which, was not too stable. The city was badly damaged by bombs, and so were the railroad track.

Surprisingly, the train was on time. He pressed the ticket into my hand, and I gave him mine. We said goodbye and boarded the train. I thought about the encounter and realized that the very young were not guilty for what their elders did.

The train was as slow as molasses. It took much longer than it should. By the time we arrived, it was quite dark. I was the only person left. I got off and took the first bridge I came to—a big mistake. That was not the one. This bridge was only for military use. It was off limits to civilians. I had to turn and walk back to where I started from. The MP man directed me to the one I had to take. I shall never forget that crossing. The bridge was nothing more than wooden planks. I had to hold on to a rope in order not to fall through.

Just as I thought that this was the worst part of the trip, I discovered that this was only the beginning. I found myself in a city that had more holes than Swiss cheese. The young German was right, there was hardly a building that was not destroyed. Luckily, I came across a policeman, the only living soul beside me. I asked him to help me. I showed him the address I had. He then told me that not in a million years would I find it myself. After walking a great distance, he stopped at a ruin of a house. It didn't look like someone could live there. I was sure that he was mistaken; Mrs. Gerhard could not live in that place. There was no way I would enter it. I was convinced that it would collapse as soon as I took the first step. The policeman left me standing. I stood there, and I called out. To my surprise, Mrs. Gerhart came through a broken door. I was never so happy to see her; she was not too happy to see me. Nevertheless, she invited me in. When I hesitated, she assured me that it would be all right. She guided me on the rickety steps. We entered into a cold room, where I could see stars—there was a huge hole in the roof.

Mrs. Gerhart was curious about my visit. After I explained why I came, she said that we would talk later. First we'd have a little nourishment. She brewed some ersatz coffee, but all she had were cookies. We sat on a bench and talked. I told her about Paul. She took it badly. I could sense that she worried about not being able to do business without him. She gave me a couple of blankets, reminiscent of my time in the camp. I went to sleep on the floor; she slept on a cot, which was the only bed she had. I was very tired from the trip and fell asleep immediately.

In the morning, she borrowed eggs from a neighbor, made coffee again, and we ate the scrambled eggs. While consuming the meager breakfast, we discoursed about the possibilities of getting in touch with Zenek. She had bad news for me. The Belgian occupiers had left the city. In the meantime, there were only Germans in charge. Seeing how disappointed I was, she said that all was not lost; we would go to the Jewish Gmina. There might be a chance that they could help. We took a trolley. I was surprised that it was operating in that ruin of a town. There were only a few buildings that escaped the destruction. Adolph Hitler did a good job for the German population.

We arrived at a structure that housed the Gmina; this one was only partially destroyed. The place seemed oddly deserted. Down a long hall, I spotted a couple of men speaking Hebrew. I asked them if they knew where I could find the director. One of the men asked what business I had with him. I began to ramble on and on about coming all the way from Frankfurt, seeking help to get my brother out of Belgium so he and I could emigrate to the United States. Frankly, I wasn't sure that they understood what I was talking about.

As I was soon to learn, one of them was indeed the man I was looking for. Unfortunately, there was nothing he could do for me. He told me what I already knew. The only Belgian man who would be able to help left the city and was on the way home, and so was he himself. It happened that the Jewish High Holiday was beginning the next day. Still, he said that there was a small chance that the Belgian Governor hadn't left yet. He would be glad to give me a ride to the town hall, which was on his way. I asked Mrs. Gerhard if she would mind if I went there. She was glad, for she had some chores to take care of.

The director let me off in front of the building and wished me luck. I walked to the main entrance. I was stopped by a German policeman. He asked who and what I wanted to see. I told him that it was imperative for me to see the Governor (he was still in). He checked the appointment list. Since my name was not on it, he would not allow me to enter. I thought of the Nazis who were fond of saying that nothing was impossible under the sun. Then I remembered the cigarettes I had in my bag. Once before they saved me, so maybe now they would work their magic and come to my rescue again. I handed the man two packs. I was amazed how well it worked. The cop turned his back to me and told me to make it fast. I ran inside and took the stairs to the first floor, where I found the office of the Governor. I walked in and was faced by a very impressive secretary.

She sat behind a huge desk. I approached her bravely and asked to see the Governor. She, too, asked if I had an appointment, to which I replied truthfully that I had not. She then told me that it would be impossible. The Governor was finished with his tasks and was on his way out. I was desperate; I would not give up. Practically in tears, I begged, but she still refused. I began to sob in earnest. Just then the door to his office opened, and the man himself came out.

He checked with his secretary to determine if all his chores were done. Then he eyed me closely, realized that I was crying, and asked why I was there. I proceeded to tell him my sad tale, leaving nothing out. He then took my hand in his and led me into his office. He sat me down and asked me to be calm as I told him all. He ordered food to be brought, and the two of us had lunch. I was famished, since I had a very meager breakfast, and I ate well. While I was talking, he made notes. Then he began to make calls. I didn't understand what he was saying; he spoke in French, but he made it a point to explain in German what he was saying. Because Steve had no telephone, he called a nearby grocery store, hoping that Helen was a customer there. He also called his wife and told her that he might be late coming home. He told me to go home to Frankfurt and assured me that he would not leave this place till he had Zenek on his way home. That wonderful man said that, most likely, Zenek would be home before me. I had no choice but to believe him and try myself to go home in time for the meeting with the consul.

I returned to Mrs. Gerhart's squalor. I told her what I accomplished and thanked her for her help. She insisted on taking me to the train depot. We crossed the dangerous bridge. She held my hand so I felt more secure. She stayed with me till the train came and I was on it.

I was mentally and physically exhausted. As soon as the train began the journey, I fell asleep. I did not wake until it pulled into the Frankfurt station. With the rest of my money, I took a taxi all the way to Zalcheim. I was surprised that the lights were on so late; maybe Irene had given birth while I was away.

The first person I saw was Zenek. I was astounded and so was he. Before I had a chance to utter a word, he began to babble. He was in a state of shock and could not comprehend what happened. He only knew that when they sat down to dinner, there was a loud knock on the door. Helen opened it, expecting the worst, always afraid of people in uniforms. In came a Belgian policeman and a woman who was also in some kind of uniform. Steve, Helen, and Zenek were sure that they came to arrest Zenek for his illegal entry into the country. Instead, they explained that they came to help him to return to Frankfurt. He had an important appointment with the American consul to be sworn in, and soon after, he would be going to the States. Next thing he knew, they were shopping for a suitcase, which the lady filled with presents for the whole family. He was given an American passport. He was to travel as a correspondent. They put him on a special express train (only for liberators) for Frankfurt. He was amazed; everything happened so fast. He knew not who was responsible for that miracle. Then I spoke and told them that it was my doing. At first, they thought that I made it up, but when I explained how I met the Governor and what a great man he was, they realized that I was not bluffing, and all of it really took place, thanks to my meeting with that gracious and wonderful human being. We sat up that whole night retelling our experiences.

43

That morning, Irene went into labor. We rushed her to the hospital, where she gave birth to a little boy. Paul was still incarcerated and knew nothing about the child, and that now he was a father. Zenek, Zosia, and I went to see him in order to give him the good news. He was not there. When we inquired about his whereabouts, we were told that he was transferred to an American jail and that he would be better off sitting with soldiers rather than in the German prison. There was one bad thing about it; we would not be able to visit him. I could not accept the fact that he was being treated like a monster, while the real ones were walking around free.

The next day, Zenek and I went to the consul, where we were sworn in and were told that within a week we would depart for America. Through the prison chaplain, we were able to let Paul know that he had a child, a precious little boy. Between visits to Irene, we were busy making preparations for our trip, when we were visited by the American CIA. It seemed that upon hearing about the baby, Paul escaped from jail. The authorities were sure that he would show up at the hospital or home. They posted undercover men at both places. Since we were unable to get in touch with him, there was no way we could warn him.

Somehow, David found out about the baby and Paul. He came back to Zelheim. Hearing of the stakeout, he became enraged. Consequently, he did something stupid. While visiting Irene, he was questioned by the agents, and foolishly he admitted that he was the father and dared them to arrest him. They did. Now we had two criminals in the family. At first we laughed and thought that it was a big joke. Unfortunately, the police didn't. They had no sense of humor. What to us was funny, to them was a serious matter. They refused to let David go and kept him in the brig. We were told that that they would let him go only if we produced Paul. How could we, when we didn't know his whereabouts. Poor David spent three days in jail. Thanks to the chaplain who intervened, he was finally released.

The night before Zenek and I were to leave, Paul showed up, completely unaware of the havoc he had caused. All he wanted was to see his wife and baby. We would not let him go to the hospital, where the G men were waiting. He was tired, so we made him lay down to rest. Afterwards, he promised that once he saw his loved ones, he would give himself up.

Less than a hour later, the police surrounded our house. They got their man, and without letting him see his family, they led him away like a common criminal. The last time I saw him, he was under arrest and led away shackled as if he were a common murderer. Our parting, which should have been joyous, turned into a nightmare. At first, Zenek and I were ready to forgo the journey, but Irene and Zosia would not hear of it. My dear cousin promised and assured us that she would care for Irene and baby.

David also had to leave. He and Jenny were expecting their baby any day, and he wanted to be near his wife for the birthing. Tearfully, we said our farewells. He left for Belgium reluctantly, and we for the Bremen port. Upon arriving there, we were told that we would be quarantined for a week, but as it turned out, we were there for almost two months. There was a strike; no ships were leaving the port. Zenek was quartered with five boys in one room and I with five girls, plus a young married couple. I knew one of the girls in the Ghetto. It was great to see her alive and be roomies. The other girls were nice enough but much older than I or my friend. Still, we had fun, especially when they explained to us that we should give a little privacy to the honeymooners. Every afternoon we would leave the room and let them know when we would return. We spent that time roaming the place; thus, we met a lot of boys from other parts of Germany.

All of us confided that we were anxious to finally leave that despised country. Nontheless, as the strike continued, I became restless. I missed Zosia and Irene. It looked like the strike was nowhere near to being settled. I longed to go back to Zelcheim. After I expressed my feelings to Zenek, he absolutely forbade me to go there. We were not allowed to leave the grounds, but as usual, that didn't stop me. I told my friend Clara that I was going back for a couple of days, and she, too, decided to join me. In the evening, the two of us found a way to sneak out. We were experts at going through the ever-present fence. Once outside, we took a train, and we were on our merry way.

It was worth the trip. Once I walked into the house, the joy in Irene's and Zosia's eyes was indescribable. It felt as if it were the first time when we met at Bergen-Belzen. I held the baby in my arms that whole day, and that new life that came into our family made me think of the new life I was about to embark on and how much I'd miss them. We talked the whole night. We made promises not to let the distance change our devotion to one another. We spoke about Paul (still in jail). Since he was interned in the American brig, he made friends with many soldiers, who upon their release from prison, traded with Irene. She became quite adept at it and was making lots of money. Most of it she spent on lawyers, trying to get Paul released. So far, no luck.

Zosia was in love and took me to meet her boyfriend. I liked that guy, and I told her so. Secretly, I hoped that this was the man for my dear Zosia.

During the short time I was gone, lots of good things happened to our friend, Hansi. She found a cousin who was in the Canadian intelligence force. That is, he found her; she never knew that she had relatives in Canada. He wrote her that he'd be in Germany for the Nuremberg trials, and would she like to attend them and meet him at the same time?

Everyone in Zelzheim was glad to see me once more. Much too soon, we had to go back. Clara and I hated to leave, but we had to return fast to Bremen before the authorities found out about our absence. Irene gave me a warm jacket for the trip. It was getting nippy, and I could use it. She packed a suitcase full of goodies, including a bottle of vodka and a few American dollars. We parted tearfully, this time for God only knows how long.

On the return trip, we ran into some difficulties. We were not aware that we had to have papers, special permits to ride on that particular American railroad. We tried to tell them that we were going to Bremen on orders from the consul. The MPs didn't buy it. Finally, I said that we were mere babies and didn't need any papers. The Military Police began to laugh, pointing at us and repeating, "babies." I didn't know how to say teenagers, so I substituted it with babies. Later on, I found that the expression "babies" was what made them laugh. Anyhow, they let us ride the train.

Upon arriving, we made our way the same as we left. Zenek was mad at me. At the same time, he was glad to see me back, and not too soon. The strike was finally over, and we were scheduled to leave on the first boat, called the SS Marine Marlin. We opened the vodka, put out the food Irene gave me, and celebrated.

Our most anticipated journey was once more postponed, no explanation and no reason given. To our dismay, we were only told that we had to wait till January, when the next boat, named after a famous correspondent who lost his life during the war, would finally take us to the States. That ship was called Ernie Paul. In the meanwhile, we were to have a New Year's party in the mess hall. Thus, we had something exciting to look forward to.

We became preoccupied with worry about clothes, as if we had a choice. If one of us had more then one dress, we shared it with another. I did have my little black one and a navy blue party dress. Clara asked if she could wear the black one. I was happy to oblige. The boys had no such problems, since most of them possessed only the suit they wore every day. The girls washed their shirts; at least they would be clean.

The time in between went quickly. We parted with some of our acquaintances, who were leaving on the first ship. We wished them luck and made promises that we would meet in the States.

December thirty-first came, and the party took place. It was a nice and festive ball. I was the most popular damsel there. The boys lined up in order to have a dance with me. At one point I became overheated and went out to cool off. It was freezing outside; I must have taken a chill. In the morning I felt very ill. One of the girls went to tell Zenek. He took me to the infirmary. There were many people waiting in line to see the only doctor there. While waiting, I fainted. The next thing I knew, I was waking up in the hospital. A much-worried Zenek sat beside me. I asked him what happened to me, thinking that it was the same afternoon. Zenek explained that four days had elapsed since I took ill. I had been in a coma all that time. Seriously sick, I had a bad case of pneumonia, and now there was no way we could board the ship. The doctor told him that it would take a long time for me to recuperate and recovery would take a couple of weeks.

In the meantime, the boat was ready for departure. Zenek was afraid that he'd have to board without me, and that once again we might be separated. I assured him that I felt well enough for the trip. Because the infirmary was short of help, no one would realize that I left.

I did as I said. I sneaked out of the hospital. That afternoon, we left on the SS Ernie Paul. The ship was originally an army transport, discarded after the war, unfit for anything except to carry the poor immigrants. Correction: there were some private and paying passengers—Germans, American citizens, who prior to the outbreak of war, left for the Fatherland, convinced that under Herr Hitler Germany would rule the world. Now, disappointed, they were returning to America. They were not ashamed or afraid to admit to those schemes. Because they were paying guests, they were given the best accommodations, unlike us, who were herded, as many as six into one small cabin. That was only the females. The boys were even worse off. They were housed in the galley. I admit that it galled me to watch those Germans, who once again were on top of the world. No one cared, and we appreciated the little crumbs that were given to us. Our spirits were soaring with each day that was taking us closer to the beautiful land of our dreams.

44

Among us, there were many talented boys and girls. There was a piano player, a violinist, a girl with the most haunting voice, even a boy that could swallow a sword or razor blades. His parents left him with a friend who worked in a circus, where the child learned his trade. Every evening, those youngsters would entertain us; that is, until the ocean became rough and we became ill with seasickness.

The ship began to take on water. The galley was the first casualty. It flooded, and the men had no place to sleep. The boys stayed in the hallways during daytime and slept on tables in the mess hall. Some shared our cabin. I had taken Zenek in to share my bunk. The social workers that chaperoned us didn't approve and constantly chased them out.

On the last leg of the voyage, the storm was raging so badly that the boat was seriously damaged. Crates of food were floating all around. I was scared that we might not make it to the promised land. The SS Ernie Paul had seen its last voyage. In spite of the horrendous weather, the limping ship made the port of New York. We passed the Statue of Liberty and learned it's famous motto, "Give me your tired, the huddled masses yearning to breath free. Give me the poor and the homeless." I thought that never before were the people who passed it on their way to America more tired, homeless, and poor than the children of war torn Europe. The children of the Holocaust.

Europe's Child

In darkness while all earth's asleep,
My tortured soul goes back in time
When men created purgatory
Committing horrors beyond endurance
Then turned to beast,
My aching heart feels none but grief.

My tender years I spent in hell
I never saw a ray of sun
or heard a robin sing
humanity was debilitated
compassion gone
all hope eliminated.

I mourn for all my loved ones gone
and shall miss forever
those tortured souls I hear at night,
that's when I wake in sweat and fright
before me lay the sacrifices
I cry in pain, oh little greedy men!
Don't let it be in vain!

By Mary Natan